RISING STARS

The 10 Best Young Players in the NBA

Glenn Nelson
Dalton Ross
Andrea Whittaker

Sports Illustrated
KiDS
BOOKS

This Library Edition First Published and Exclusively Distributed by
The Rosen Publishing Group, Inc.
New York

For my inspiration — Sassia, Mika, and Florangela. For my vision — Mom and Dad.
— Glenn Nelson

For Christina — my wife and WNBA fan extraordinaire — for everything she does for me, each and every day. — Dalton Ross

For Meredith Hale and Gary Sussman. — Andrea Whittaker

This library edition first published in 2002 and exclusively distributed by The Rosen Publishing Group, Inc., New York

Copyright © 2002 SPORTS ILLUSTRATED FOR KIDS Books

Book Design: Michelle Innes
Additional editorial material: Eric Fein and Nel Yomtov
Originally edited by Ron Berler
Photo credits: Cover, (left) © Icon Sports Media, (center) © Gerald Raube/Icon SMI, (right) © Icon Sports Media; Introduction page, chapter start pages and background images © Photodisc; pp. 7, 71, 109, 125, 131, 137 © Reuters New Media Inc./CORBIS; p. 13 © Duomo/CORBIS; pp. 21, 33, 35, 47, 63, 103 © AFP/CORBIS; pp. 27, 49, 79 © Icon Sports Media; pp. 43, 81, 89, 93 © ALLSPORT; pp. 55, 65, 139 © Manny Millan/SI/Icon SMI; pp. 95, 111 © John W. McDonough/Icon SMI; pp. 117, 123 © Steve Lipofsky/Icon SMI; p. 147 Mark Cowan/Icon SMI

First Edition

Library of Congress Cataloging–in–Publication Data

Nelson, Glenn.
Rising stars : the 10 best young players in the NBA / by Glenn Nelson, Dalton Ross, and Andrea Whittaker.
    p. cm.
"Sports illustrated for kids books."
Includes index.
Summary: Sports biographies of ten outstanding current players in the National Basketball Association.
  ISBN 0-8239-3574-4
  1. Basketball players--United States--Biography--Juvenile literature. 2. Basketball players--Rating of--United States--Juvenile literature. [1. Basketball players.] I. Title: 10 best young players in the NBA. II. Ross, Dalton. III. Whittaker, Andrea. IV. Title.

GV884.A1 N46 2002
796.323 ' 092 ' 273--dc21

                                                        2001004383

CONTENTS

INTRODUCTION	4
KOBE BRYANT	6
TIM DUNCAN	20
STEPHON MARBURY	34
ALLEN IVERSON	48
VINCE CARTER	64
KEITH VAN HORN	80
JASON KIDD	94
JASON WILLIAMS	110
SHAREEF ABDUR-RAHIM	124
KEVIN GARNETT	138
CAREER STATS	152
GLOSSARY	156
RESOURCES	157
INDEX	159

INTRODUCTION

When Michael Jordan retired before the 1998–99 season, many basketball fans wondered if any player would ever capture their heart again. If you have watched basketball since then, you know the answer is *yes!* There are great young players blossoming all over the NBA.

Los Angeles Laker guard Kobe Bryant reminds fans of former Laker great Magic Johnson, while high–flying Toronto Raptor guard/forward Vince Carter makes eye-popping dunks like Michael's. San Antonio forward Tim Duncan sparked the Spurs to the 1999 NBA title. And forward Kevin Garnett of the Minnesota Timberwolves has simply changed the way his position is played!

But there's more. Slick guards Allen Iverson, Jason Williams, Stephon Marbury, and Jason Kidd make moves that spectators can hardly believe. Forwards Shareef Abdur-Rahim and Keith Van Horn are turning heads, too.

In *Rising Stars*, you'll learn about all 10 players. You'll discover the challenges they faced and overcame. You'll learn about their secret dreams and happiest days. Most of all, you will learn about the heart and dedication that it took for them to succeed — in basketball and in life.

KOBE BRYANT

In a city of stars, he shines the brightest

Kobe Bryant has star written all over him. It's in the sly, cocky smile that plays on his face. It's in the gold of his Los Angeles Laker home uniform, which he wears like a royal robe.

Most of all, it's in the elegant way he flies to the basket, as if he were a 6-foot-7, 215-pound Olympic gymnast, dazzling even his opponents with his moves. He makes the game look so easy. He will flick his hand in front of a rival to steal a pass, then score on a move so smooth that he leaves fellow players shaking their heads in disbelief.

Kobe is the youngest player ever to start an NBA game and the youngest ever selected to play in the NBA All-Star Game. He did both before he was 20

statcity

KOBE BRYANT

TEAM	Los Angeles Lakers
POSITION	Guard
ACQUIRED	Drafted No. 13 overall by Charlotte Hornets, in 1996, and traded to Los Angeles Lakers for Vlade Divac
BORN	August 23, 1978, in Philadelphia, Pennsylvania
HEIGHT	6' 7"
WEIGHT	215 pounds
HIGH SCHOOL	Lower Merion (Pennsylvania)
CAREER BESTS	51 points (against Golden State, 12-6-00), 6 steals (twice)
HONORS	NBA All-Star, 2001, 2000, 1998; All-NBA Second Team, 2000-01; NBA All-Defensive Second Team, 2000-01; NBA All-Defensive First Team, 1999-2000; All-Rookie Second Team, 1997

years old. "It's like a dream come true," Kobe said.

He's right — it *is* a dream, of sorts. But it's a dream that came true because of years of hard work. Work that not even his teammates always see. Kobe still pretty much lives in the gym. He is still improving. How good can he be? "I'm just getting started," he said.

GROWING UP IN ITALY

Kobe was born August 23, 1978, in Philadelphia, Pennsylvania. His father, Joe "Jellybean" Bryant, was a smart, hard-nosed forward who played for the Philadelphia 76ers, the Houston Rockets, and the San Diego Clippers over eight NBA seasons, from 1975 to 1983. When Kobe was 3 years old, he would play along with a Nerf ball and mini-basket while watching his father play on TV.

"Right away, he started dunking," Kobe's mother, Pam, recalled. "I said, 'Sweetheart, you'll break the basket. Don't dunk. Just shoot jump shots and layups.' He'd have his little cup of Gatorade and his towel, and he'd say, 'Mom, I'm sweating.' "

Joe's NBA career ended when Kobe was 5. But Joe didn't want to stop playing. He accepted an offer to join a pro team in Italy. He and Pam decided that living in Europe would be a great learning experience — not only for them, but also for Kobe and his two older sisters, Shaya and Sharia.

The family spent eight years in Italy. Kobe loved it there. He learned to speak Italian fluently, and he excelled in school. In his free time, he devoted himself to basketball. He followed his father's career, of course, but he practiced and studied the game largely on his own.

Kobe spent hours studying tapes of Los Angeles Laker games. Most of the tapes came by mail from his grand-parents, in the U.S. Kobe's favorite player was Magic Johnson, who helped lead the Lakers to five NBA titles. Magic was a sky-walking acrobat who played with energy, passion, and sheer joy. Kobe tried to play like that.

"I watched Magic and [Boston Celtic star forward Larry] Bird, Michael [Jordan], and Dominique Wilkins [a top forward nicknamed The Human Highlight Film]," Kobe said. "They added to my game. That's where all the creativity came from. I would imagine myself playing against somebody and doing a move I saw them do on videotape."

HIGH SCHOOL PLAYER OF THE YEAR

In 1991, when Kobe was 13, his parents decided to return to Philadelphia. Joe and Pam wanted to enroll their children in American schools, to prepare them for college in the U.S.

At first, Kobe didn't fit in. "I was the little kid with the Italian accent and the Italian game," he said. But he start-ed adding some street moves to his game — for instance, 360-degree spins to glide past defenders. They won him acceptance and admiration from the other kids.

In 1992, Kobe entered Lower Merion High School, in Ardmore, Pennsylvania. Kobe knew by then that he wanted to be a pro basketball player. The first time Coach Gregg Downer saw him play, he knew Kobe was special. "After five minutes, I said 'This kid is going to be a pro,' " Coach Downer said. "Never was there one moment I doubted that."

Kobe made the varsity team his freshman year. By the time he was a junior, he had made a local name for himself. In 1995–96, his senior season, he led Lower Merion to a 31–3 record and its first state championship in 53 years. Kobe scored 50 points in one game! He averaged 30.8 points, 12 rebounds, 6.5 assists, 3.8 blocks, and 4 steals per game for the season. By the end of his high school career, Kobe had replaced NBA great Wilt Chamberlain as the top high school scorer in Southeastern Pennsylvania history.

But it wasn't just Kobe's game skills that set him apart. "He's a motivator," said Rob Schwartz, one of his high school teammates. "Even though he was the best player on our team, he always worked hard. One time, he broke his nose at practice. He got up, and with one eye closed, shot with his left hand and hit a three-pointer. It was amazing."

After the season, Kobe was named by both *USA Today* and *Parade* magazine as the nation's High School Player of the Year. He was also selected to the McDonald's All-America Team. A number of top colleges recruited him, including Duke University, the University of Michigan, and the University of North Carolina.

A DREAM COME TRUE

But since ninth grade, Kobe's goal had been to do what only four players had ever done, up to that time: jump from high school directly to the NBA. Three retired years ago — Moses Malone, Darryl Dawkins, and Bill Willoughby. Only Kevin Garnett was currently playing. All four were big men. No guard had ever before made that leap. At the time, Kobe was a 6-foot-5 guard.

But Kobe had a second goal. His two childhood heroes, Magic and Michael, had returned to the NBA. "I wanted to get in the league and play against those guys," he said.

Kobe's parents believed that Kobe was good enough — and mature enough — to play in the NBA. So on April 29, 1996, Kobe announced that he would enter the 1996 draft. Los Angeles Laker general manager Jerry West was interested. He invited Kobe to Los Angeles and put him through a series of drills. Jerry, a Hall of Fame player, knows talent. When Kobe finished, Jerry said, "He's simply the best prospect who ever worked out for us."

The Lakers struck a draft-day deal with the Charlotte Hornets. Charlotte made Kobe the number 13 pick overall and immediately traded him to Los Angeles for center Vlade Divac. Not only was Kobe in the NBA, he was playing for his favorite team!

Kobe Bryant

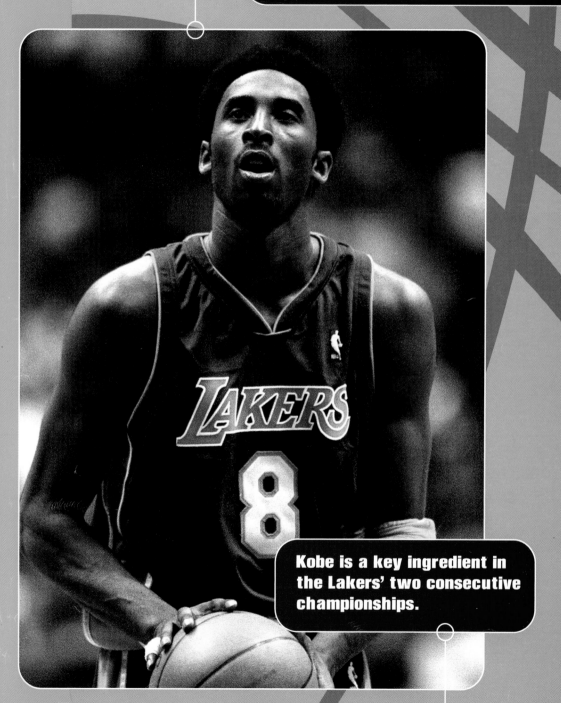

Kobe is a key ingredient in the Lakers' two consecutive championships.

Hall of Fame DOUBLE

Like Magic Johnson, the Lakers' joyous, acrobatic star of the 1980's and 1990's, there is something about Kobe that sets him apart from other players and makes it hard not to like him. Growing up, Kobe studied tapes of Magic's games for hours. He watched Magic's ball-handling skills, shooting touch, and personality and built them into his own game. Like Magic, too, Kobe is a tall guard who can play almost any position on the court.

A ROOKIE'S UPS AND DOWNS

Kobe was barely 18 years old when the 1996–97 season began. He spent much of the early part of the season on the bench. Laker coach Del Harris knew that Kobe was an excellent ball handler who could shoot from almost anywhere. And he could leap above taller players to dunk. But Kobe was still learning how to be more of a team player, and Coach Harris didn't want to rush him. The coach's philosophy played an important role in the development of the future superstar.

Slowly, Kobe started getting more court time. On January 28, 1997, against the Dallas Mavericks, he became the youngest player ever to start an NBA game. He was 18. He caught everyone's attention during the 1997 NBA All-Star Weekend, when he won the slam-dunk contest and scored 31 points in the Rookie All-Star Game. Shaquille O'Neal watched Kobe's performance closely that weekend. When asked how good Kobe could become in the future, Shaq said: "It's going to be scary....It's going to be *real* scary."

By playoff time, Kobe was playing close to 20 minutes per game. He was so athletic that he played three different positions: point guard, shooting guard, and small forward. Coach Harris began to turn to him in clutch situations.

But in a crucial game in the second round of the playoffs, Kobe shot four air balls in the closing minutes against the Utah Jazz. The Lakers lost, ending their season. Kobe felt that he was to blame. It was the type of experience that can rattle a player's confidence. Many around Kobe — including Magic Johnson — were curious to see how the young player would respond.

It didn't take long to find out. A few hours after the team returned to Los Angeles, Kobe walked into the gym. "That was just like me," Magic said. "This is where he needs to be." Said Kobe, "Those air balls didn't bother me. Give the ball to me right now in that situation, and I'd take a shot again." In fact, Kobe did just that. In his first trip back to Utah the following season, he blocked what would have been a game–tying shot by one of the Jazz players. Then he made a memorable dunk to win the game.

In 1998, Kobe became the youngest player ever selected to the All–Star team. He finished the 1997–98 season averaging 15.4 points per game, more than double the 7.6 points per game he averaged in his rookie season.

LEARNING NEVER STOPS

By 1998–99, Kobe's third season, Michael Jordan had retired and Kobe had replaced him as the NBA's most popular star. Again, he helped lead the Lakers to the playoffs, averaging 19.9 points per game. And again, the Lakers lost, this time to the San Antonio Spurs, who went on to win the title. Kobe decided he had to work even harder.

When former Bull coach Phil Jackson was named the Lakers' new boss, in June 1999, Kobe was one of the first to call him. "Teach me the game," he told Phil. "Teach me what I don't know."

NBA CHAMPS

Phil had the experience to turn the Lakers from a contending team into a championship team. He had led the Chicago Bulls to six NBA titles by getting players to work together and play as a team. Learning to play as a team would change the Lakers' fortunes.

Phil came into a situation where there was a lot of tension. Both Kobe and Shaq wanted to lead the Lakers in his own way. Shaq believed that since he had more experience, Kobe should follow his lead. Kobe thought that Shaq should focus on defense and leave running the offense to him.

Phil worked to get the players to put aside their differences for the good of the team. "Kobe didn't have a selfish agenda; he just felt that the way he had been playing was the best way he could contribute," he said. Eventually, the tension faded into the background and winning an NBA championship took center stage.

The Lakers stormed through the 1999–2000 regular season as Kobe put up career-high numbers. He averaged 22.5 points, 4.9 assists, and 6.3 rebounds per game. In the 2000 Finals against the Indiana Pacers, Kobe was forced to miss Game 3 with a badly sprained ankle. In Game 4, however, he came back to score 28 points and the game–winning basket in overtime. "This was the game I dream about every day," he said. Kobe's contribution to the Lakers' quest for the championship wasn't over. In Game 6, Kobe poured in 26 points, helping the Lakers capture their first NBA title since 1988.

A POOR START

Kobe and the Lakers were as surprised as everyone else when they got off to a slow start in 2000–01. They lost their first three games of the preseason, causing many people to wonder what the problem was. Many people blamed Kobe, saying that he was taking too many shots and not looking to pass off to his team-mates. Shaq agreed.

It looked like the tensions between the two stars would derail the Lakers from another championship run. But the players' desire to win another NBA title helped get the team to improve its playing. As the weeks passed, the Lakers started to dominate on the court as they had the previous year.

On a personal note, Kobe got the 2000–01 season off on a flying start. In December 2000, he was chosen the NBA Player of the Month. He earned this honor by aver-aging 32.3 points, 4.8 rebounds, and 4.9 assists per game.

Kobe continued to be one of the most popular players in the league. He received the most votes for his position in the All-Star team balloting. In the 2001 All-Star game, he led his Western Conference teammates with 19 points and 7 assists but lost to the East, 111–110. Kobe's performance was memorable, but he and the Lakers had their eyes on a bigger goal — winning a second straight NBA title.

Kobe ended the 2000–01 season with even more career highs. He averaged 28.5 points and 5 assists per game.

On one memorable night against the Golden State Warriors, he scored a career-high 51-points.

A GREAT FINISH

The Lakers easily made it to the playoffs again and tore through their opposition. In the first round, they swept the Portland Trail Blazers. In the conference semifinals, they swept the Sacramento Kings. In the conference finals, they swept the 1999 champion San Antonio Spurs. No team in history had dominated its playoff opponents as the Lakers were doing.

The only bump in the Lakers' path to the championship was a surprising Game 1 overtime loss to the Philadelphia 76ers in the Finals. After that, it was a smooth ride. In Game 5, Kobe scored 26 points to help the Lakers take the series and the NBA championship. He averaged 24.6 points, 7.8 rebounds, and 5.8 assists per game in the Finals as the Lakers posted an astonishing 15-1 playoff record on the way to the title.

As he's become one of basketball's hottest young stars, Kobe has grown as a player and person. Everyone's noticed it. Phil said, "I think he's mature beyond his years....I think he's grown a lot...."

Kobe's a practical young man who knows how to keep things in perspective. "Basketball is kind of like life," Kobe stated. "You can get knocked on your butt. But you have to get up and hold your head high and try again. That's how I'm going to be."

TIM DUNCAN

He doesn't need to yell and shout. His game says it all.

While his San Antonio Spur teammates celebrated madly on court, Tim Duncan raced for his video camera. The Spurs had just won the 1999 NBA title and Tim wanted to document the moment. "I'm keeping it on tape," he said. "It's a blessing to get where I am now."

Who could blame Tim for wanting to preserve this special moment? He had led the Spurs to the title, averaging 27.4 points and 14 rebounds per game during the five-game Final series with the New York Knicks. It was the Spurs' first title in the team's 32-year history. For Tim, it was the crowning moment in

his journey from being a shy, clumsy kid from a small island to being the Number One player in the world.

Tim was born April 25, 1976, on the island of St. Croix, in the U.S. Virgin Islands. (The Virgin Islands are in the Caribbean Sea, near Puerto Rico.) By age 13, Tim was already a great athlete. But his main sport was swimming. His whole family — which included a brother and two sisters — were swimmers. Tim had hardly played basketball.

Tim was a top freestyle swimmer. His older sister, Tricia, went on to swim for the Virgin Islands in the 1988 Olympics. "Timmy was even better than me," Tricia said. "There is no doubt in my mind that he would have gone to the 1992 Olympics and held his own against the world."

But then, on September 17, 1989, Hurricane Hugo hit St. Croix. The storm destroyed the only Olympic-sized pool on the island. Tim's swim team was forced to hold practices in the ocean. "Tim was not happy about swimming in the ocean," his father, William, said. "He was afraid of the sharks." So he gave up the sport.

MR. CLUMSY

For awhile, Tim had no special sport. That changed a year later. Tim's mother, Ione, died of breast cancer. Tim's older sister Cheryl and her husband, Ricky Lowery, moved back to St. Croix from Ohio to help care for the family. Ricky got Tim interested in basketball, partly to help get Tim's mind off his mother's death.

There were only four indoor basketball courts on the entire island, but Tim and Ricky practiced on them constantly. At first, Tim was so awkward with the ball that Ricky nicknamed him Mr. Clumsy. Tim improved slowly. But he *grew* quickly. While he was a student at St. Dunstan's Episcopal High School, he grew eight inches, to 6-foot-9.

Tim's big break came in the summer of 1992, when he was 16. A group of NBA rookies had come to the Virgin Islands to help promote basketball. Tim got to play in a game with Alonzo Mourning, who went on to become the star center for the Miami Heat. Tim performed so well that another of the touring players told his college coach about him. The college was Wake Forest University, and the coach was Dave Odom. Coach Odom soon flew to St. Croix. He watched Tim play and immediately offered him a scholarship.

A PROMISE TO HIS MOTHER

Tim had grown to 6-foot-10 and 200 pounds by the start of his freshman season at Wake Forest. But since he had played basketball for just a few years, he was still rough around the edges. In his first game, against the University of Alaska at Anchorage, Tim went scoreless. He didn't even attempt a shot.

TIMOTHY THEODORE DUNCAN

TEAM	San Antonio Spurs
POSITION	Forward
ACQUIRED	Drafted No. 1 overall by San Antonio in 1997
BORN	April 25, 1976, in St. Croix, U.S. Virgin Islands, an island near Puerto Rico
HEIGHT	7'
WEIGHT	248 pounds
COLLEGE	Wake Forest University
CAREER BESTS	46 points (against Utah, 1-10-00), 23 rebounds (twice)
HONORS	NBA All-Star, 2001, 2000, 1998; All-NBA First Team, 2000-01, 1999-2000, 1998-99, 1997-98; NBA All-Defensive First Team, 2000-01, 1999-2000; NBA Finals MVP, 1999; NBA Rookie of the Year, 1997-98

But Tim was a quick and eager learner. In his sophomore season, he scored 16 points and grabbed 20 rebounds to help lead Wake Forest to an upset win over the University of North Carolina. The victory gave Wake Forest its first Atlantic Coast Conference tournament title in 32 years.

"He learned faster than anyone I've ever coached," Coach Odom said. Tim averaged 19.1 points and 12.3

rebounds per game in his junior year, and was named the ACC Player of the Year. Had he wanted, he could have left college then for the NBA. Most experts said he would have been the number one pick and could have pocketed millions of dollars. But Tim chose to remain at Wake Forest.

One reason he stayed was that he had promised his mother he would graduate from college. The other was that he simply loved being at Wake Forest. "I was having fun in college," Tim said. "And I was still growing up."

In his senior year, Tim simply dominated on the basketball court. He became the first player in ACC history to lead the conference in scoring, rebounding, field-goal percentage, *and* blocked shots, all in one year. His combination of size, strength, speed, and shooting skill earned him several national player-of-the-year awards.

TEAMING WITH DAVID ROBINSON

The San Antonio Spurs were thrilled that Tim had stayed in school. The Spurs had been one of the league's best teams during the 1990's, but they had tumbled to a 20–62 record in 1996–97 because of injuries. David Robinson, their All-Star center, missed almost the entire season due to back and foot injuries. The Spurs ended up with the number one pick in the 1997 NBA draft, and they chose Tim. There was more good news: By the start of the 1997–98 season, all their players, including David, were healthy.

The Spurs knew that Tim had talent, but even *they* were surprised by his skill. Shortly after the draft, David invited Tim to his Colorado home to practice. He was amazed by Tim's technique. "He's everything he was advertised to be," David said. "But what I didn't expect was his tremendous passing. Wow!"

On offense and on defense, Tim could do it all! He had grown to be 7 feet and weighed 248 pounds. That made him strong enough to play close to the basket. But he also had a nice, soft shooting touch from outside. Michael Jordan, for one, was impressed. In Tim's third NBA game, he went head–to–head with Michael and the NBA champion Chicago Bulls. Tim scored 19 points and grabbed 22 rebounds. Afterward, Michael said, "I can see why he went number one [in the draft]. He stayed those four years in college and the payoff for doing that is starting to show."

Tim had one of the best rookie seasons in NBA history. He averaged 21.1 points, 11.9 rebounds, and 2.5 blocked shots per game. He was the third player ever to be named Rookie of the Month for all six months of the season, and was named the NBA Rookie of the Year.

More important, Tim teamed with David to form a combination that made the Spurs a powerhouse. In Tim's first year, San Antonio improved its record by 36 wins — the biggest jump in NBA history! In the playoffs,

Tim Duncan

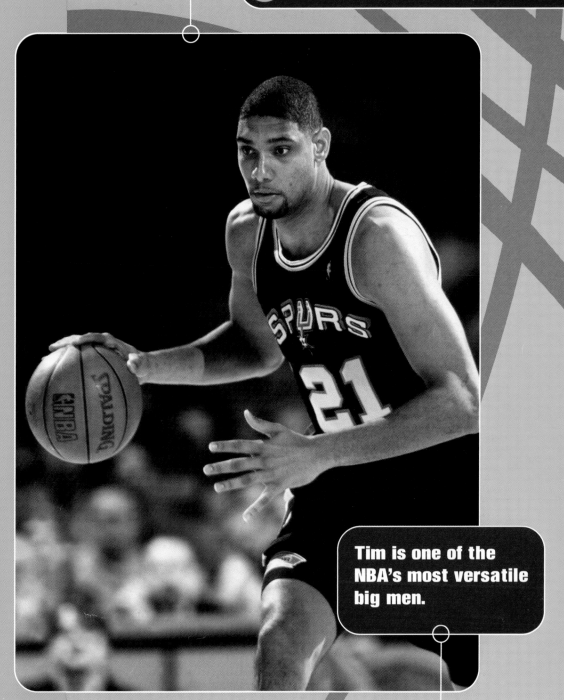

Tim is one of the NBA's most versatile big men.

Hall of Fame DOUBLE

Kareem Abdul-Jabbar was the greatest center of the 1970's and 1980's. He led the Milwaukee Bucks to one championship and the Los Angeles Lakers to five more. Like Kareem, Tim does his job quietly, with a minimum of fuss. He is strong and quick, and often uses Kareem's favorite weapons: the jump hook shot, the skyhook, and the power move inside. Both stayed in school and earned their college degrees.

the team advanced all the way to the Western Conference semifinals, before losing to the Utah Jazz.

THE ROAD TO THE NBA FINALS

Still, people questioned Tim's ability to lead the Spurs to the next level, the NBA Finals. After 14 games in the 1998–99 season, the team was a disappointing 6–8. Critics wondered about Tim's passion to win. Even one of Tim's teammates, Mario Elie, questioned his desire. Tim waited until after the season to respond.

Tim had majored in psychology in college. He said he had taken what he had learned about how people's minds work and used it in his game. "If you show disappointment or frustration [on the court, and] your opponent picks up on this, you are at a disadvantage," he wrote in *Sport* magazine. "I make sure opponents don't know what's going on in my head."

In a league filled with emotional show-offs, Tim is a throwback. "It's uncommon for someone his age to be so competitive, yet poised," Spur coach Gregg Popovich said.

Teammate Will Perdue agreed. About the only time Tim shows emotion, Will said, is when he's "kicking somebody's behind in Sony PlayStation."

Led by Tim, the Spurs recovered from their 6–8 start. They went 31–5 the rest of the season. Tim was spectacular. He beat teams under the basket. He beat them from outside, with his skyhook and bank shots. He beat them on defense with quick feet and an intimidating presence. He averaged 21.7 points, 11.4 rebounds, and 2.5 blocks per game, and finished third in voting for the league's Most Valuable Player. But Tim's regular-season play was nothing compared to what he would do in the postseason.

In the opening round of the playoffs, Tim and the Spurs made quick work of the Minnesota Timberwolves.

Then they swept the Los Angeles Lakers in four games. Tim averaged 29 points and 10.8 rebounds per game. Next, the Spurs swept the Portland Trail Blazers.

"THE BEST PLAYER IN THE NBA"

Tim had led the team to its first–ever NBA Finals, against the New York Knicks. The Spurs won that series, four games to one. Tim was named the MVP of the Finals. He averaged 23.2 points, 11.5 rebounds, and 2.6 blocks per game over the course of the playoffs.

"He's obviously the best player in the NBA," Knick coach Jeff Van Gundy said afterward. "You can just watch a guy play and know if he's truly into winning or not. That guy's truly into winning."

All the swimming practices, the discipline and deter–mination, the basketball lessons from Ricky, the four years of college ball: They had all finally paid off. Tim was now a champion and Mr. Clumsy was no more.

ANOTHER CHAMPIONSHIP RUN

Tim carried his winning ways into the 1999–2000 season. He finished the season with averages of 23.2 points, 12.4 rebounds, 3.2 assists, and 2.2 blocks per game. He was only one of two players to rank among the top ten in scoring, rebounds, and blocks. Tim was named to the All–NBA First Team and the NBA All–Defensive First Team for the second year in a row. He was also named the co–MVP of the 2000 NBA All–Star

Game, sharing the honor with Shaquille O'Neal.

Injuries kept Tim from playing the full 82–game schedule. In late February and early March, he missed four games due to a lower abdominal strain. He made his way back into the lineup, but in a game against the Sacramento Kings on April 11, Tim tore the cartilage in his left knee. He missed the last four games of the season and the entire playoffs.

Although Tim did everything he could to return to action in time for the playoffs, his teammates didn't want him playing if it meant risking further injury. Teammate David Robinson said, "I know he's dying to play, but if you can't run, you can't play. It's just that simple." Sadly for Tim and his teammates, the Spurs were knocked out of the playoffs in the first round. The Phoenix Suns took the best–of–five series 3–1.

On May 24, Tim had surgery to repair his knee.

BACK TO WORK

In the off–season, Tim re–signed with the Spurs, to the delight of teammates and fans. The Orlando Magic tried to sign him, but lost out in the negotiations. On his decision to stay with the Spurs, Tim said, "When it came down to it, I just liked what I had here."

In good health, Tim played in every Spurs game of the 2000–01 season. On the year, he averaged 22.2 points, 12.2 rebounds, and 3 assists per game. For the third straight year, he made both the All–NBA First Team and the NBA All Defensive First Team. With Tim at the helm, the Spurs ran up the best regular-season record in the NBA with a mark of 58–24.

In the Western Conference finals, the Spurs faced the defending NBA champion Los Angeles Lakers. Tim played well, averaging 23 points and 12.3 rebounds per game. But the powerhouse duo of Shaq and Kobe was too much for the Spurs. The Lakers swept San Antonio in four games. Tim was disappointed but gracious about being disqualified from the series. He said of the Lakers, "They played incredibly. They were better in the series; they always seemed to have an answer for us."

OFF-THE-COURT EXCELLENCE

With or without another championship ring, Tim's off-the-court charity work rivals his game performances. In the last two years, he has raised money for many good causes. In January of 2000, he hosted the first annual Tim Duncan Bowling for Dollars Charity Bowl-A-Thon. It raised over $100,000 for the American Cancer Society. During the 2000 season, Tim also worked with Sprite and Ultramar Diamond Shamrock to create the Beat Cancer program. It raised $50,000 for the Cancer Therapy and Research Center in San Antonio.

In 2001, Tim was awarded the Home Team Community Service Award by the NBA and Fannie Mae Foundation, an organization dedicated to improving housing conditions. The award recognized Tim's help in rebuilding inner-city neighborhoods throughout the country. "As an NBA player and role model, I feel a responsibility to support the community that supports my team," he said.

Tim's sense of responsibility — on the court and off — has taken him a long way, from a child swimmer in St. Croix to one of the NBA's brightest young stars.

 In 1999, Tim led the Spurs past everyone to their first-ever NBA title.

STEPHON MARBURY

The hardest-working player in the NBA

S tephon Marbury lives in a nice home in a pleasant neighborhood these days. Every so often, though, he returns to his family's old apartment in the Coney Island section of Brooklyn, New York.

Up four flights of dirty stairs and down a dark, cinder–block hallway is the simple home that the Phoenix Suns' star point guard lived in when he was growing up. Getting his family out of that 15–story Surfside Garden housing project is what drove Stephon to make it to the NBA.

A few years ago, Stephon moved his parents far from Coney Island, to a quiet Maryland suburb. But

the Marburys still keep the apartment in Surfside Garden. And Stephon keeps going back to Brooklyn to visit it. Returning to the apartment reminds Stephon of where he has come from. It reminds him how hard he worked to get out of Surfside Garden and how hard he must work to continue to be one of the most electrifying players in the NBA.

"I'm always going to come back," said Stephon. "It helps keep me real, no doubt."

TALENT ISN'T ENOUGH

Stephon was born February 20, 1977. He is one of seven children. His father, Donald, Senior, was a construction worker who sometimes couldn't find work. His mother, Mabel, worked in a day-care center. There was never much money. Stephon had three older brothers. The family's dream was that one of the brothers would make it to the NBA and help them escape poverty.

The oldest Marbury brother, Eric, was 17 when Stephon was born. He came close to making the NBA. He was a hard-nosed guard who played at the University of Georgia, with future NBA star Dominique Wilkins. But Eric was cut by the San Diego Clippers during training camp, in 1982. He couldn't catch on with any other teams. So he moved back to Brooklyn and became an ironworker. And he started coaching his younger brothers, hoping one of *them* would make it.

"Maybe I wasn't good enough," Eric said. "But ever

since my brothers were small, I made sure they all knew the commitment it would take for them to make it."

Eric worked first with Donald, Junior, called Donnie, and then with Norman, known as "Jou–Jou." They didn't make the NBA, either. Their chances were hurt when poor grades cost them big–time college scholarships. Donnie, a shooting guard, eventually played two years at Texas A&M University. Jou–Jou, a point guard, played one season at St. Francis College, in Brooklyn.

Three Marbury brothers had come out of Brooklyn's Abraham Lincoln High School billed as superstars. All had failed to make it to the NBA. The family began to get a reputation of being underachievers. Eric didn't want Stephon to be another Marbury underachiever. Luckily, Stephon shared his brother's fierce determina-tion to succeed.

BROTHER KNOWS BEST

Anybody could see that Stephon had talent. When he was 3 years old, his father took him to the University of Georgia to watch Eric play. During a team practice, he scampered out to center court, picked up a ball, dribbled it to the basket, and laid it in. At age 9, he was performing shooting exhibitions during halftime at Lincoln High's games. When he turned 11, *Hoop Scoop*, a national basketball magazine, named him the best sixth–grade player in the country!

Eric developed a strict training program for Stephon.

▶ STEPHON XAVIER MARBURY

TEAM	Phoenix Suns
POSITION	Guard
ACQUIRED	Traded to New Jersey from Minnesota as part of a three-team trade, March 11, 1999; traded to Phoenix from New Jersey, June 28, 2001
BORN	February 20, 1977, in Brooklyn, New York
HEIGHT	6' 2"
WEIGHT	180 pounds
COLLEGE	Georgia Tech University
CAREER BESTS	50 points (against Los Angeles Lakers, 2-13-01), 20 assists (against Indiana, 4-25-99)
HONORS	NBA All-Star, 2001; All-NBA Third Team, 1999-2000; NBA All-Rookie First Team, 1996-97

Each day after school, Stephon ran sprints along Coney Island's beach, then raced three times up and down the 15 floors of his apartment building.

Part of his training was doing well in school. Stephon was determined not to be derailed by poor grades, as Donnie and Jou–Jou had been. He never questioned Eric's plan. "I knew everything he told me would make me better," Stephon said. Like all his brothers, Stephon wore Eric's uniform number, 3.

MR. NEW YORK BASKETBALL

By the time Stephon entered Lincoln High, in 1991, he was one of the most talked about prospects in New York City basketball. The skills that would eventually carry him to the NBA were already developing — the startling quickness, the excellent ball–handling skills, the deadly accurate jump–shooting, the terrific passing ability.

Stephon lived up to his billing. For three straight seasons, he led the school to the city's championship game. In 1994–95, his senior year, he averaged 28 points, 9.5 assists, and 3.5 steals per game. In the title game, Stephon scored 26 points — including two game-clinching free throws with 11 seconds remaining — to lead Lincoln to a 61–56 victory.

There was more. Two weeks later, Stephon scored 28 points to lead Lincoln to its first state high school championship. He was named a *Parade* magazine High School All–America, and Mr. New York Basketball!

That fall, in 1995, Stephon enrolled at Georgia Tech University. He started his freshman season with a bang. In his first game, he scored 16 points to lead Georgia Tech to a win over Manhattan College, despite battling tonsillitis and a 102–degree fever. "Stephon doesn't walk on water," said Fran Frashilla, Manhattan's coach at the time, "but he doesn't get very wet, either."

Against Georgetown University and its standout guard Allen Iverson a few days later, Stephon turned heads with his quickness and his no–look passes. He had 13 points, 8 assists, and 7 steals. Stephon led the Yellow Jackets to the Atlantic Coast Conference title, averaging a team-high 18.9 points per game. He became just the fifth freshman in ACC history to be selected to the All-Conference team! Stephon was named a third-team All-America.

STEPHON AND KEVIN

Soon after the season ended, Stephon announced that he would leave Georgia Tech and enter the 1996 NBA draft. Milwaukee selected Stephon number four overall and traded him the same day to the Minnesota Timberwolves. Stephon was ecstatic. A Marbury had finally made it! His family wept with joy.

Stephon couldn't believe his good fortune. He already had a friend on the Wolves: Kevin Garnett. The two had played together during high school on the U.S. Junior National Select Team. For several years, they had phoned each other regularly to talk about their NBA dreams. Now they would be teammates. Together with top-scoring forward Tom Gugliotta, they would be something.

Stephon was only 19 years old, but he proved himself almost immediately. In December 1996, he put on a dominating performance against All-Star guard John Stockton and the Utah Jazz, with 33 points and 8 assists. For the season, he averaged 15.8 points and 7.8 assists per game and finished second to Allen Iverson in voting for 1997 Rookie of the Year. More important, he helped lead the Wolves to the playoffs for the first time in franchise history.

The following season, 1997–98, Stephon performed even better. He averaged 17.7 points and 8.6 assists per game. That year, the NBA All-Star Game was played in his hometown, New York City. Stephon thought he would be selected for the game. But he wasn't. That failure made him think about the short distance that separated Madison Square Garden from his family's poor Brooklyn apartment. Stephon decided to work at his game even harder.

GOING HOME

After the All-Star Game, Stephon went on a tear. He averaged 26.2 points over the next six games! He helped carry the Wolves back to the playoffs.

In Game 2 of the first round, against the Seattle SuperSonics, Stephon put on the best performance of his career. He scored 25 points, had 7 assists, and made 2 steals to lead the Wolves to a 98–93 win, their first playoff victory! Minnesota won another game before being eliminated.

Stephon and the Wolves seemed one solid player away from becoming one of the NBA's elite teams. But it wasn't to be. Instead, Tom Gugliotta left after the season to play for the Phoenix Suns. With Tom gone, Minnesota decided to rebuild completely. On March 11, 1999, as part of a three-team trade, the Wolves sent Stephon to New Jersey.

Stephon had always dreamed of playing near home. Now he was back, close to his Brooklyn roots. His happiness showed in his game. On April 25, 1999, against the Indiana Pacers, he had a career-high 20 assists. Ten days later, playing the Milwaukee Bucks, he scored a career-high 41 points. He finished the 1998–99 season averaging 21.3 points per game — eighth best in the NBA. He ranked third in assists, with 8.9 per game.

After the season, Stephon signed a long-term contract with the Nets. Stephon's dream was to win the NBA title with a New York City–area team.

GREAT EXPECTATIONS

Stephon and the Nets had high hopes as they began the 1999–2000 season. With guard Kerry Kittles, forward Keith Van Horn, and Stephon, the Nets had a trio of players who could shoot and score. Unfortunately, the team got off to a slow 2–15 start. They missed center Jayson Williams, who was on the sidelines recovering from a broken leg. "We had a rocky start. Guys were kind of in a funk, all of us. We were trying to find ourselves as a team. We didn't establish our identity at the beginning of the season and that hurt us," Stephon said.

Stephon blossomed into an All-Star player with the New Jersey Nets.

Hall of Fame DOUBLE

Stephon is one of the NBA's top passers and scorers. Only one other point guard in NBA history had that combination of talents: Hall of Famer Nate "Tiny" Archibald. Tiny played for seven teams in the 1970's and early 1980's. Like Stephon, he was blindingly quick, and was a master of the no-look pass. Tiny was the only guard ever to lead the league in both scoring and assists in the same season. If anyone can match that feat, it's Stephon.

Despite the Nets' poor showing, Stephon had another outstanding season as he led the team with a 22.2–points–per–game average. His 8.4 assists per game ranked him 7th in the NBA. For his efforts, Stephon was selected for the All–NBA Third Team.

Things didn't improve much the following year as the Nets' woes continued in the 2000–01 season. The team fell to a 26–56 record, down from the 31–51 mark they posted in 1999–2000. Once again, however, Stephon had a big year. He notched a career-best 23.9 points per game while averaging 7.6 assists per game. He put up his first career triple-double against the Chicago Bulls. In that game, he scored 33 points, dished 12 assists, and grabbed 11 rebounds.

AN ALL-STAR PERFORMANCE

One of Stephon's season highlights was his stellar performance in the 2001 All-Star Game, which was his first appearance in the mid-season classic. Stephon scored 12 points, had 4 assists, and sank the game-winning shot, as he led his Eastern Conference teammates to a thrilling come-from-behind 111–110 victory. Stephon said, "It felt good. It couldn't have worked out better. Two three-pointers to help my team win the game? I'll be telling my kids about that some day!"

Stephon's solid 2000–01 showing came despite a ruptured tendon in his left pinkie that he suffered in mid-January. By the end of March, the pain was too much for him to ignore. "It was getting to the point where the pain was unbearable because I have been getting hit on it so much," he said. "It's tough to play with a pinkie that's curled up." Stephon missed 15 games and underwent surgery to repair the damage.

THE IMPORTANCE OF FAMILY

Off the court, Stephon puts in a lot of time toward worthy causes. He hosts several fund-raising events himself and helps other celebrity athletes with their charitable work. He's dedicated many of his efforts to helping children with disabilities and underprivileged kids and their families.

Family is an important part of this rising young star's life. Regarding his family coming to see him play, Stephon said, "Having my family here, and every night knowing I have fifteen to twenty people coming to see me play, that just keeps me humble; not as a player, it keeps me humble as a person. You always have someone saying 'You need to do this,' or 'You should have done that.' I'm not the type of guy who dislikes criticism. I love criticism. It keeps me on my toes."

A CHANGE OF SCENERY

On June 28, 2001, Stephon was traded to the Phoenix Suns for Jason Kidd in a blockbuster deal. At first Stephon had doubts about the trade, but he soon accepted the idea and became optimistic about the move to a contending team. "I think I can win a championship with this team. This will make my career go through the roof."

Stephon has made his mark on the NBA and proven himself to be one of its top new stars. But he's still not comfortable. He still thinks of his family and all their years of struggle. So even now, he keeps returning to the apartment in Brooklyn. It is a reminder of what his life would have been like without hard work and dedication. All he has to do is walk past the courts he played on as a kid to be reminded of all the players out there who are hungrier than he is.

"I work harder now at my game than I did two years ago, because I understand that now people are going to be gunning for me," he said. "Every minute I'm not working, someone's lifting weights, someone's running, someone's shooting jump shots. That's why I can't stop."

▶ **Even against bigger players, Stephon refuses to lose.**

ALLEN IVERSON

Looking for excitement? Here's "The Answer."

He has been called "The Answer," but Allen Iverson has spent most of his career raising questions. He has raised questions in other people's minds about his attitude, his judgment, and his values. In his first two NBA seasons, the Philadelphia 76er guard was arrested once, suspended by the league once, and disciplined by his team a number of times. Michael Jordan and other great players called him a selfish hotshot who would not listen to coaches.

Many considered it a shame that Allen's attitude and behavior were getting in the way of so much talent. Because, clearly, he is one of the most exciting athletes ever to play the game. He is the most acrobatic scorer since Michael. Though he is just six feet

ALLEN IVERSON

TEAM	Philadelphia 76ers
POSITION	Guard
ACQUIRED	Drafted No. 1 overall by Philadelphia in 1996
BORN	June 7, 1975, in Hampton, Virginia
HEIGHT	6'
WEIGHT	165 pounds
COLLEGE	Georgetown University
CAREER BESTS	54 points (against Cleveland, 1-06-01), 15 assists (twice), 9 steals (against Orlando 3-19-00)
HONORS	NBA All-Star, 2001, 2000; All-NBA First Team, 2000-01, 1998-99; All-NBA Second Team, 1999-2000; NBA Rookie of the Year, 1996-97; First Team All-America, 1995-96

tall, he is a ferocious dunker. His passing and ball handling are dazzling. "He's so quick, he leaves his teammates behind," said basketball Hall of Famer Dave Bing. "I don't even know that *he* knows how fast he is."

But Allen played for himself, and his team seldom won. Then, in 1999, he changed his act. Allen stopped

getting into trouble. He showed up on time for practice
— and made sure his teammates did, too. He listened
more carefully to his coach. Instead of always looking to
shoot the ball, he began to pass to his teammates and
involve them in the game. For the first time, Allen led
the Philadelphia 76ers to the playoffs. *Surprise!*

Allen had matured. At last, he seemed to be squarely
on his way to a Hall of Fame career.

A FOOTBALL FAN

Allen's path to the NBA wasn't easy. He grew up
extremely poor in Hampton, Virginia. He was born June
7, 1975, the year his mother, Ann, was 15 years old. His
father deserted the family soon afterward. His stepfather
was in and out of jail. Allen remembers nights when he,
his mother, and his sisters, Brandy and Liesha, had no
running water or electricity in their home.

For Allen, sports were an escape from his family's
struggles. He threw himself into every game he played.
A good player, he was determined to become a professional athlete so that he could help improve their lives.

Growing up, football was Allen's favorite sport. "Still
is," he said. "I didn't even want to play basketball at first.
I thought it was soft. My mother's the one who made
me go to tryouts. I'll thank her forever."

At Bethel High School, in Hampton, Allen starred at
both. He led the school to the state football title, playing

quarterback and safety. That winter, he led Bethel to the state basketball title, too! Colleges recruited Allen for both sports.

TROUBLE AND TRIUMPH

Then Allen ran into his first trouble with the law. On the night of February 14, 1993, Allen walked into a bowling alley in Hampton, just as a wild fight broke out. Dozens of people were involved. Allen said he left the bowling alley as soon as the fight began, but two witnesses said he was one of the brawlers. He was found guilty at a trial and sentenced to five years in jail.

But Allen got a second chance. Virginia Governor L. Douglas Wilder re-examined the case. Governor Wilder found no evidence against Allen. After serving four months in jail, Allen was released, and the guilty verdict was dropped.

Questions about his reputation remained. Few colleges wanted to take a chance on Allen. But after a long talk with him, Georgetown University basketball coach John Thompson decided to offer him a scholarship. Allen responded by leading the 1994–95 Hoyas with 20.4 points and 4.5 assists per game. He was named the Big East Conference's Rookie of the Year and Defensive Player of the Year.

That's when Allen picked up the nickname The Answer. Fans started calling him that because he seemed to have a solution for any problem on the court.

A special bond formed between coach and player. Coach Thompson had been a father figure to other Georgetown stars, such as Patrick Ewing, Dikembe Mutombo, and Alonzo Mourning. Now he took Allen under his wing. "He taught me a lot of things: how to deal with people, how to deal with different situations," Allen said. "It made me feel good that he was comfortable with me. That meant a lot to me."

Allen played even better during his sophomore season. He averaged 25 points, 4.7 assists, and 3.35 steals per game, and led Georgetown to the 1996 NCAA tournament. After the season, he was named a First Team All-America. He was the best point guard in college basketball!

Allen could have remained at Georgetown. But fewer than 150 miles away, his family was still living in poverty. He decided to enter the 1996 NBA draft.

ADVICE FROM MICHAEL

The Philadelphia 76ers had the first pick in the 1996 NBA draft. At 6 feet and 165 pounds, Allen became the shortest number one selection in the history of the draft.

His effect on the team was immediate. In Allen's first NBA game, he scored 30 points against the Milwaukee Bucks. Defenses just couldn't keep up with him. After trying — and failing — to cover Allen, guard Ron Harper said, "I thought I could play defense. Now I don't know."

Unfortunately, Allen's cockiness and bad attitude were just as evident as his talent. After his hot start, he began showing up late for practice. He rarely passed the ball to his teammates. All Allen cared about, it seemed, was scoring. This rubbed a lot of players the wrong way.

During the 1997 All-Star Weekend, Michael Jordan, Patrick Ewing, and Charles Barkley urged Allen to change his attitude. But Allen wouldn't listen. Late in the season, he set an NBA record by scoring 40 or more points in five straight games. He did it shooting almost every time he got the ball, seldom passing. The 76ers lost all five games. Though Allen averaged 23.5 points per game for the season and was named Rookie of the Year, Charles Barkley was unimpressed. He called Allen "me, myself, and Iverson."

That summer, Allen got into some real trouble. Police stopped his Mercedes for speeding. Allen wasn't driving, but he was in the car. The police searched the vehicle and found marijuana and a handgun. Allen was charged with drug and firearm possession. The charges were later dropped, after Allen agreed to perform community service and undergo monthly drug tests for two years.

ALLEN'S NEW TEACHER

Allen had been lucky to find John Thompson. Now, he got lucky again. In 1997, Larry Brown was hired as the new 76er coach. Coach Brown had been a star point

Allen Iverson

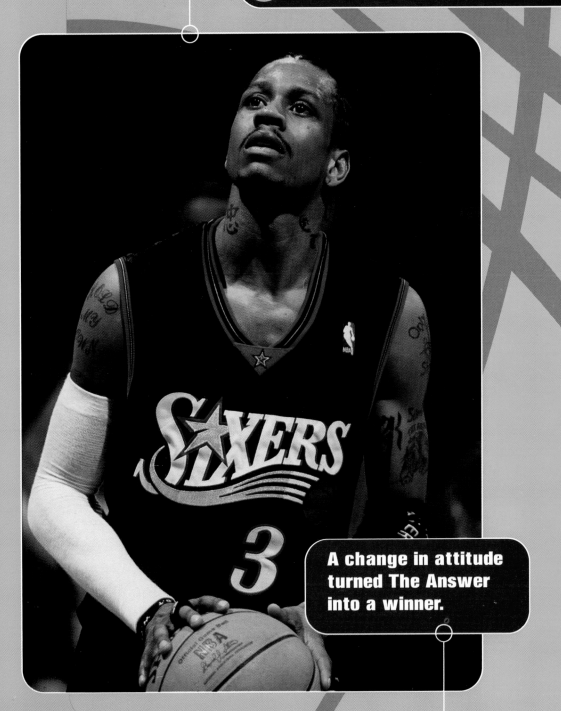

A change in attitude turned The Answer into a winner.

Hall of Fame DOUBLE

Allen is an undersized guard with phenomenal speed, super passing ability, and the guts of an NFL running back when driving to the basket. What Hall of Famer does that sound like? Isiah Thomas, who helped the Detroit Pistons win two titles, in 1989 and 1990. In addition, Isiah and Allen both started at point guard and sometimes shifted to shooting guard. Both were great scorers. Isiah was the first player from Indiana University to leave college early for the NBA. Allen was the first Georgetown player to leave school early.

guard in the old American Basketball Association before he turned to coaching in 1972. After his playing days, Coach Brown became one of basketball's most successful head coaches. He coached the Carolina Cougars and the Denver Nuggets to ABA championships in the 1970's. In following years, he coached the Bruins at UCLA, the New Jersey Nets, and the University of Kansas Jayhawks, where he won the NCAA Championship in 1988. In following years, he coached the San Antonio Spurs, the Los

Angeles Clippers, and the Indiana Pacers. By the time he came to Philadelphia, he had won over 1,000 games. As a coach, his strength is teaching team–oriented basketball. He made Allen his special project.

Coach Brown tried to teach Allen what Chicago Bull coach Phil Jackson had taught a young Michael Jordan: that great players make their *teammates* better. But Allen grew frustrated when he made a good pass and his teammate missed the shot. He would sulk. He would report late to practice. The team disciplined him a number of times.

Slowly, though, Allen came around. And once he started passing the ball more, the number of his turnovers went way down. For the 1997–98 season, Allen averaged 22 points, 6.2 assists, and 2.2 steals per game. His game was becoming more complete.

But the 76ers won only 31 games in 1997–98. So over the summer, Allen decided to be even less selfish with the ball. When the 76ers gathered to begin practice for the 1998–99 season, they saw a new Allen. Coach Brown's lessons had begun to take hold.

A TRUE TEAM PLAYER

For the first time, Allen began acting as a team leader. "I think it's my responsibility to make sure guys get in here for practice, and I will," Allen said. "I want to be here when this whole thing turns around, so that I can say I've been here and suffered and now it's my turn to shine."

Shine, he did. Coach Brown moved Allen from point guard to shooting guard. The switch freed Allen to do what he does best — find ways to score. He discovered that he could open up opportunities for himself and his teammates by passing and moving without the ball. During the first month of the season, Allen led the 76ers to an 8–5 record. It was the team's first winning month in five seasons.

Allen's new team–oriented approach helped carry the team to its first playoff appearance since 1991. He also led the NBA in scoring by averaging 26.8 points per game. He was the first 76er to win the scoring title in 30 years.

But the party wasn't over. Philadelphia faced the heavily favored Orlando Magic in the first round of the playoffs. In Game 3, with the series tied at a game apiece, Allen scored 33 points and made an NBA playoff–record 10 steals. The 76ers won, 97–85. "I sent a message to my teammates that it's not just about scoring points," Allen said afterward. "That's something the coach has been working with me on."

Allen then scored 37 points to lead the team to a 101–91 Game 4 victory that clinched the series! Coach Brown was proud. "Allen's doing what great players do," he said. "He's making other people better, and he is taking responsibility."

In the Eastern Conference semi-final round, Philadelphia lost the best-of-seven series to the Indiana Pacers, 4-0. The 76ers were done for the season, but Allen's growth as a player and a person promised good things to come for the team and its fans.

A CLASH OF PERSONALITIES

Unfortunately, the fans would have to wait a while longer for the good things. The 76ers got off to a disappointing 5-8 start in 1999-2000. The team was playing inconsistently and tensions were beginning to rise between Allen and Coach Brown. Coach Brown was upset with Allen's choice of shot selection, and Allen was disappointed that he had been moved to point guard again. There were even rumors of Allen being traded to another team. Finally, in December, emotions came to a head when Coach Brown benched Iverson in a game against the Detroit Pistons.

"Everybody's got to execute, everybody's got to share the ball, and everybody's got to defend. That's not happening," said Coach Brown after the benching.

Allen was displeased and expressed his frustration. "For some reason, my style doesn't fit this team [any] more. So I need to get out of here. It's as simple as that," Allen said. A few days later, Allen apologized for his remarks and said that he wanted to continue playing in Philadelphia.

Allen and Coach Brown patched up their differences, and the team started to roll. Allen's 28.4 points–per–game average during the regular season made him the second leading NBA scorer behind Shaquille O'Neal. Allen was selected as a starter in the 2000 NBA All–Star Game. He dazzled the crowd, as he scored a high of 26 points and dished 9 assists. The 76ers finished the season with an impressive 49–33 record and made the playoffs once again.

In the first round, Iverson — playing with a bad ankle and injured elbow — led the 76ers to a first–round series win over the Charlotte Hornets. Allen scored 44 points in the Game 4 series–clinching finale. In the next round, the 76ers met the Indiana Pacers again. As they did in 1999, the Pacers knocked the 76ers out of the playoffs. Indiana took the Eastern Conference semifinals, 4–2.

INCHING CLOSER TO A CHAMPIONSHIP

During the summer of 2000, once again, talk heated up about trading Allen — this time to the Los Angeles Clippers. The 76ers feared that the problems between Allen and Coach Brown would recur in the 2000–01 season. The trade was never made. Allen vowed to change. Before the season began, he asked Coach Brown to let him be the team's co-captain. Brown agreed. The decision was a good one.

The season began with Allen and Coach Brown getting

along very well. A fast 7–0 start by the 76ers was proof that things were going right between them. Allen's desire to lead his team was strong. "It will be important for me to send that message to my teammates by being the first guy there [practice and games] and the last to leave," he said. Coach Brown was very happy with Allen's hard work and commitment. He said, "He's been great. He's practicing better. I'm proud of him."

The year was to be the team's best performance in 18 years. Allen led the league in points (31.1), steals (2.5), and minutes per game (42). He also scored a career–high 54 points in a game against the Cleveland Cavaliers. Allen was also named the NBA Player of the Month for January 2001.

Allen's 25–point performance in the 2001 All–Star Game earned him the game's Most Valuable Player award. When he was presented with the award by NBA commissioner David Stern, Allen asked, "Where's my coach at? Where's Coach Brown?" Allen's question showed just how far the two men had come in under–standing and respecting each other.

As a crowning achievement, Allen was the NBA's MVP for the regular season. Even opposing teams raved about Allen's talent. Pat Riley, coach of the Miami Heat, said, "He is having an outrageously great year. He is no longer a work in progress. He is a work of art. He is impossible to guard. You just hope he misses."

The 76ers finished first in the Atlantic Division and headed into the playoffs looking to win the NBA championship. They made it to the Finals against the defending champions, the Los Angeles Lakers, despite being hobbled by injuries. The 76ers managed a Game 1 overtime victory behind a 48–point performance by Allen, but the Lakers swept the next four games to hold onto the title.

A disappointed Allen said, "It's been a long tough year. I'm 165 pounds, I've been beat up all year, and I just thank God I'm able to play." In the Game Five finale, played in Philadelphia, he was given a standing ovation by the sellout crowd. As he left the court at the end of the game, they chanted, "MVP! MVP!"

Coach Brown paid Allen the highest compliment when he said, "He had a phenomenal year. And I think being in this environment, on this stage, people really recognize what an unbelievable competitor he is and what a great player [he is] . . . we would've never been in this position had it not been for his unbelievable play throughout the whole year."

Critics who had questioned Allen's character earlier in his career had their "Answer." Allen Iverson had made it.

Allen's blinding quickness allows him to rise above the rest of the league.

VINCE CARTER

Call him Air Canada. He's the NBA's new king of the dunk.

It was one of those all-star charity games of summer, where NBA players strut their stuff for a few minutes and then shuffle back to the bench. The host, Seattle SuperSonic star Gary Payton, played briefly. So did Magic Johnson, Penny Hardaway, and most of the rest.

But Vince Carter, the 1999 NBA Rookie of the Year, refused to leave the court. Late in the fourth quarter, the slender, 6-foot-7 guard/small forward sprinted upcourt and drilled home a 360-degree dunk. He followed that with a ringing, between-the-legs tomahawk jam. Then he delivered a scissors-kick slam. The

10,000 fans at Seattle's Key Arena leaped to their feet. The players on court responded, too. Even the opposing team wanted to see him slam.

In a league of dunking royalty, Vince is the new king. In Toronto, they call him Air Canada. "I have never seen anyone who can elevate above the rim [of the basket] like he can," said legendary NBA coach Chuck Daly. That's quite a statement from the man who coached Michael Jordan and the Dream Team in the 1992 Olympics!

Vince averaged 18.3 points per game in 1998–99, the best among NBA rookies. He knows he has been blessed with special skills. "From day one in the NBA," Vince said, "I felt that I was very capable and was here for a reason."

FLORIDA'S MR. BASKETBALL

Vince was born January 26, 1977. His mother, Michelle Carter–Robinson, and stepfather, Harry Robinson, were school teachers. Together with Vince and his younger brother, Christopher, they lived in a comfortable house in Daytona Beach, Florida. The weather there was warm enough to play outdoors year round, so Vince did! He remembers playing with a basketball at age 2.

Sports were always a big part of his life. But they weren't his whole life. Back then, Vince wasn't sure he had a future in the NBA. At 14, he was cut from his

Amateur Athletic Union basketball team. The coach told him he was too slow. So, Vince worked hard to develop other, non-sports skills in which he could excel. At Daytona Beach's Mainland High School, he wrote poetry and helped compose the school's homecoming song. He was also a drum major and saxophone player in the school marching band. Vince was so good at playing the sax that he was offered a music scholarship at Bethune-Cookman College, in Daytona Beach.

Then, the summer between 10th and 11th grades, Vince grew six inches. His world changed. Almost overnight, he became one of the best high school athletes in the entire state! He was a top volleyball player and a star quarterback on the football team. During his senior year, he was named Florida's Mr. Basketball.

Vince was amazing at basketball. In one game, he scored 47 points. In another, he blocked 17 shots. Once, he injured the wrist of his right hand, his shooting hand. What did he do? He scored 32 points left-handed! Vince led his team to its first state championship in 56 years and was named a high school All-America. He leaped so high that fans started calling him U.F.O., short for Unidentified Flying Object!

TRYING TO BE LIKE MIKE

Like a million other basketball wannabes, Vince dreamed of being like Michael Jordan. In high school,

statcity

VINCE LAMAR CARTER

NICKNAME	Air Canada
TEAM	Toronto Raptors
POSITION	Guard/Forward
ACQUIRED	Drafted No. 5 overall by Golden State in 1998, then traded to Toronto for Antawn Jamison
BORN	January 26, 1977, in Daytona Beach, Florida
HEIGHT	6' 7"
WEIGHT	215 pounds
COLLEGE	University of North Carolina
CAREER BESTS	51 points (against Phoenix, 2-27-00), 15 rebounds (against New Jersey, 3-16-99)
HONORS	NBA All-Star, 2001, 2000; All-NBA Second Team, 2000-01; U.S. Olympic Men's Basketball Team, 2000; All-NBA Third Team, 1999-2000; NBA Rookie of the Year, 1999; Second Team All-America, 1997-98

he asked to wear Michael's number 23, but a teammate already had it. Vince was heartbroken. His mother told him: "You pick another number and make it famous." That's when Vince chose number 15, which he wears today.

More than 70 colleges approached Vince to play basketball for them. Following in Michael's footsteps, he chose the University of North Carolina. In many ways, Vince seemed like his hero (*see box, page 72*). His splashy style of play and the way he carried himself off the court reminded people of the former Chicago Bull star.

Like Michael, Vince is soft-spoken, polite, and considerate. As a child, he would give away clothes he had outgrown to needy friends. "It was Vince's way of giving," his mother said.

Unlike his idol, though, Vince was *not* an instant college star. Part of the problem was that Vince had never bothered to learn the fundamentals of the game — how to pass, how to play defense, how to move without the ball. He had depended on his high-flying skills. Vince soon learned that at the college level, those weren't enough. During his freshman year, he averaged just 7.5 points per game.

"He didn't understand that there's more to the college game than scoring and out-jumping everyone else," said Dean Smith, North Carolina's coach at the time.

Vince worked for hours, daily, on his game. Sure enough, in his sophomore year, he averaged 13 points per game and was named to the NCAA East Regional All-Tournament team.

GREAT PLAYER, BETTER PERSON

As a junior, Vince emerged as one of the top college players in the country. He led the Atlantic Coast Conference in scoring, with an average of 15.6 points per game. In the semifinal game of the NCAA tournament, he scored 21 points against the University of Utah. Still, the Tar Heels lost, 65–59. Afterward, Wake Forest University coach Dave Odom called Vince "the closest thing there is to a human highlight film in college basketball."

Vince decided that he had learned all he could at the college level. He left school to enter the 1998 NBA draft.

On June 24, 1998, the Golden State Warriors made Vince the number five pick overall. Then they traded him to the Toronto Raptors for Antawn Jamison, one of Vince's North Carolina teammates, plus cash.

Toronto coach Butch Carter knew Vince was a good player. But he didn't realize what a good person Vince is. Vince arrived in Toronto not with a gang of friends, but with a group that included his minister. He wears no tattoos or earrings. He still turns to his parents for advice. "You know right away he's not cut from the same mold as most professional athletes," said his minister, the Reverend August Sorvillo.

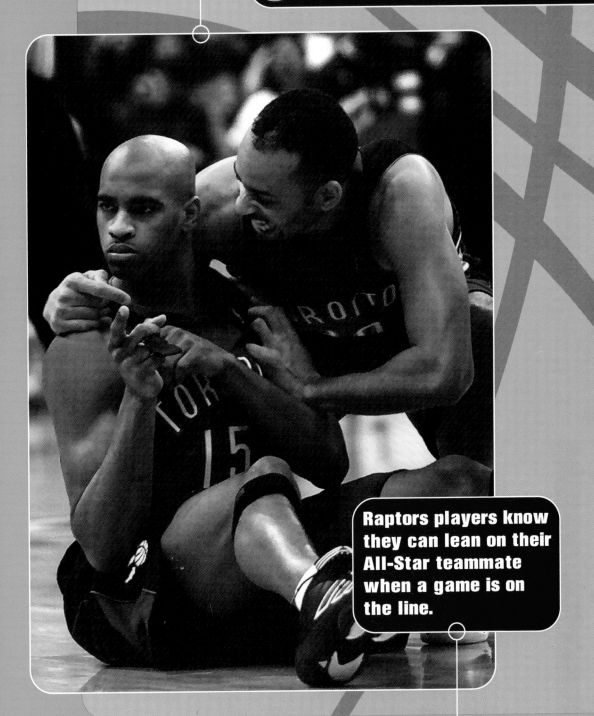

Raptors players know they can lean on their All-Star teammate when a game is on the line.

Hall of Fame DOUBLE

Vince and Michael Jordan both attended the University of North Carolina, and were named NBA Rookie of the Year. Both could fly above the rim like nobody else in the game! But Vince and Michael weren't perfect. Each worked hard to become a top defensive player. Each entered the league lacking a great jump shot. Michael developed one of the best. Vince plans to do the same.

WELCOME TO THE NBA!

Vince's pro debut, on February 4, 1999, was sensational. In his first game, against the Boston Celtics, he scored 16 points and grabbed three rebounds to lead Toronto to a 103–92 win!

But Vince's real test came on March 25, 1999, when the Raptors played the Rockets in Houston. There, Vince would go against Scottie Pippen, a seven-time All-Star and one of the best players in the NBA. "My assistants were saying that Pippen was going to kick Vince's butt," Coach Carter said. "So I started calling Vince's room, saying Scottie was going to send a limo to pick him up and make sure he got to the game [so that he could beat Vince]." In other words, Coach Carter was challenging Vince.

Vince responded in a big way. With Scottie guarding him, Vince scored 32 points. By the end of the game, Scottie was asking his teammates to help guard Vince.

Less than a week later, Vince beat the Indiana Pacers almost single-handedly. He had 31 points, 11 rebounds, and 6 assists — and scored the game-winning basket with 18 seconds left! The Raptors won, 88–87. "I think I had a lot of confidence from then on," Vince said afterward.

That's when the comparisons with Michael really began. Vince is about the same size as Michael, and he has Michael's huge, soft hands and tremendous upper-body strength. His powerful, slender legs give him Michael-like liftoff. People who have seen them both play say that Michael had better hang time, but that Vince jumps higher.

By the end of the 1998–99 season, Vince was the league's newest sensation. Fans debated Vince's greatest slams. There was his ferocious dunk over Miami's Alonzo Mourning, the 1999 NBA Defensive Player of the

Year, the body–bump–and–dunk over the game's best shot–blocker, Atlanta's Dikembe Mutombo, and the breakaway 360–degree throw–down against the Cleveland Cavaliers in the Raptors' final game of the season. No one could decide which was best.

Vince's gravity–defying acts were so numerous, the Raptors created a special video–highlights library on their website, www.raptors.com. It's called the Vince Carter Jam Cam.

In a 1999 CNN–TV poll, fans named Vince the NBA's most exciting player. It's easy to see why. Vince was the only rookie to lead his team in scoring. (He averaged 18.3 points per game.) He led all guards and small forwards in blocked shots, with 1.54 per game. He was the first Raptor ever to be named NBA Player of the Week, and he won the league's Rookie of the Year award! Most important, he led the team to its best record ever and to the edge of its first playoff berth. The Raptors fell short by just four games.

VINCE'S SUMMER SCHOOL

During the 1999 off–season, Vince kept more than busy. He had promised his mother that he would return to the University of North Carolina to earn his degree. So, he went back to campus for summer classes. He expected to receive his degree in African–American Studies, with a minor in communications, in 2000.

Vince also attended another summer-school program all his own. He wanted to improve the one weakness in his game. Like Michael early in his career, Vince lacked a great jump shot. So, he held his own private class. Each day, he took at least *1,000* jump shots. "Some days, I might shoot 1,500," he said.

"Once he can make that 18-footer, he may be impossible to stop," Pacer coach and Hall of Famer Larry Bird said.

SOPHOMORE SENSATION

Vince's performance in the 1999–2000 season showed that his private classes had paid off. In addition to his career-best 25.7 points-per-game average, he was named Player of the Week twice during the season. In a game against the Phoenix Suns on February 27, he scored a career-high 51 points. A few weeks later, Vince nailed his first career triple-double in a game against the Cleveland Cavaliers. In the game, he scored 31 points, pulled down 11 rebounds, and handed off 10 assists. He was selected for the 1999–2000 All-NBA Third Team.

Vince was an easy pick as a starter in the 2000 All-Star Game. He scored 12 points in the game, but it was his high-flying performance in the Slam Dunk competition that got all the attention. Vince likes to put on a show for the fans, but he wants to be known for more than just his flair for dunking. "Dunkers come and go. You can go down to the playground and find a bunch of guys who can do fancy dunks. The great players excel at all aspects of the game. That's what I want to do," he said.

Even though Vince was showing himself to be a genuine one-of-a-kind star, the comparisons between he and Michael continued. Vince wanted to express his own individuality: "Am I tired of [the] Jordan questions? Yeah. It's a great compliment, but everybody in the league has flashes of playing like Mike sometime. I'm more interested in establishing my own identity."

A HISTORIC FIRST

Vince accomplished one of his biggest goals of the season when the Raptors made it to the playoffs for the first time in their history. They went up against a veteran New York Knicks team who swept the young Raptors in three straight games of the best-of-five opening round.

Vince's NBA season was over, but he wasn't done playing basketball for the year. He played in the 2000 Summer Olympic Games in Sydney, Australia, on the United States' Dream Team. The team rolled to a gold-medal victory behind Vince's team-leading scoring performances in the critical semifinal (18 points) and gold-medal games (13 points). Dream Team teammate Allan Houston of the New York Knicks spoke highly of Vince. "When you can take over a game on the Dream Team, come into a pressurized situation like that, and make it happen, you've got to respect him. And I think [Vince] gained a lot of people's respect," Houston said.

SWEET REVENGE

The 2000–01 season was one of more improvements for Vince. He topped his previous year's scoring average with a 27.6 points–per–game mark — good enough for fifth best in the NBA. He was selected again as a starter at the All–Star Game.

With a strong 47–35 record during the regular season, the Raptors made it to the playoffs. Once again, their first–round opponents were the Knicks. The memory of the 2000 sweep was still fresh in the minds of the Raptors, but Vince brought the right attitude to the rematch. "The most important thing is wanting to win. We're not out here to prove anything. Maybe if we had the same team as last year we might have something to prove, but it's a whole new team. All that stuff happened last year," he said.

The Raptors shocked the Knicks. Vince led his team to a thrilling best–of–five games series win, averaging 22.8 points–per–game average. The Raptors next faced the Philadelphia 76ers in the Eastern Conference semifinals. Vince was on fire in the best–of–seven series, but even his 30.4 points–per–game average wasn't enough. The 76ers won the final game by one point and eliminated the Raptors 4 games to 3.

GRADUATION CONTROVERSY

The Philadelphia series had its moments of controversy — on and off the court. Hours before Game 7, Vince left to take care of an important matter — namely, graduating from college! Vince had earned his degree in African-American Studies from the University of North Carolina — one year later than he had planned — and he wanted to attend graduation ceremonies. He was criticized by people who thought that he should have stayed with the team, but Vince explained, "In my opinion, graduation day is one of the most important days in someone's life. You've worked so hard to accomplish this goal and today is the day you can say, 'I did it.'"

For Vince Carter there will be many more years of accomplishing his goals and doing it in a style that only Air Canada can.

Vince reminds people of his idol, Michael Jordan.

KEITH VAN HORN

He looks like a Boy Scout, but he's one tough dude

Keith Van Horn's New Jersey Nets were desperate for a win. They had already lost 10 of their first 12 games of the 1998–99 season. Now, the Nets were in danger of losing again.

The Nets were playing the Boston Celtics, in Boston. With 7.2 seconds left in the game and the score tied at 97, New Jersey guard Eric Murdoch launched a jump shot. He missed! If the Celtics were to grab the rebound, they would get the ball and a chance to set up the winning shot. The Nets would lose *again*.

But Keith didn't let that happen. The big forward grabbed the ball and dribbled to the baseline. Then,

looking as if he had all the time in the world, Keith calmly put up a short jump shot. The ball bounced twice above the rim and fell through the net. The Boston crowd fell silent. The Nets went berserk. They had won, 99–97!

Keith never once doubted that the ball would go in. That coolness under fire is what made Keith the leader of the New Jersey team in his NBA rookie season. Nothing seems to fluster him.

"He wants the game–winning shot," said John Calipari, who coached the Nets during Keith's first two seasons. "There are not many veteran players in this league who want to take that responsibility."

NBA DREAMS

Taking responsibility has been the theme of Keith's life. His parents raised him that way. "They are my role models," he said.

Keith was born October 23, 1975, in Fullerton, California, a Los Angeles suburb. He grew up in nearby Diamond Bar. Keith's father, Ken, owned a fire sprinkler company. His mother, May, stayed at home and cared for Keith and his older brother and sister, Jeff and Kim.

"My father was always a calm and collected person," Keith said. "He never really let anything bother or upset him. He was never a yeller or anything like that. So I guess I kind of got him in my personality."

Keith's passion for basketball began early. By age 8, his dream was to play in the NBA. On weekends and during the summer, he shot hoops from sunrise to sunset. Then he would go home and watch Los Angeles Laker games on television. His bedroom walls were covered with posters of NBA stars Magic Johnson, Michael Jordan, and Larry Bird.

Keith never tried to pattern his game after those players, though. He was smart enough to know that he lacked Larry's court vision, Magic's ball-handling skill, and Michael's jumping ability. Instead, he worked with the tools he had — quickness, strength, smarts, and speed.

"Every player establishes his own individuality in a game," Keith said. "To me, basketball is the most creative of all sports. You never see the same play twice. Just like a musician who has the freedom to make whatever music he wants, a basketball player has the freedom to create moves."

OUTSMARTING HIS OPPONENTS

At age 13, Keith stood 5-foot-10. He started playing in summer leagues in Los Angeles. He sought out the best playground games in the city. Though he looked more like a Boy Scout than an intimidating player, Keith was no pushover. He beat big players with up-and-under moves around the basket and tossed in jump shots over leaping defenders. He outsmarted opponents with head

statcity

KEITH VAN HORN

TEAM	New Jersey Nets
POSITION	Forward
ACQUIRED	Drafted No. 2 overall by Philadelphia in 1997, acquired by New Jersey in an eight-player trade
BORN	October 23, 1975, in Fullerton, California
HEIGHT	6' 10"
WEIGHT	250 pounds
COLLEGE	University of Utah
CAREER BESTS	35 points (against Detroit, 2-16-99), 18 rebounds (against Washington, 11-7-99)
HONORS	NBA All-Rookie First Team, 1997-98; First Team All-America, 1997

fakes that left them grabbing air, and broke to the basket with a first step that was so quick they barely saw it.

By Keith's sophomore year at Diamond Bar High School, he had grown to be 6–foot–9. In his senior year, he dominated his league. Keith averaged 29.2 points, 10.1 rebounds, and 3.7 blocks per game and was named to the All–Western United States high school basketball team.

Keith enrolled at the University of Utah, largely because of Coach Rick Majerus. "Coach Majerus is a disciplinarian," Keith said. "But at the same time, he really cares for his players. He doesn't have children, so in some sense, we're kind of his kids and he looks after us."

Coach Majerus taught Keith NBA–style basketball. That meant learning set offensive plays and man–to–man defense. Keith flourished. As a freshman, he led the team with 18.3 points per game. He also ranked in the Top 10 among players in the Western Athletic Conference (WAC) in scoring, rebounds, 3–point goals, and blocked shots.

SETTING PRIORITIES

But it wasn't an easy year for Keith. Midway through the season, his father died of heart failure. Keith was devastated. "It's hard to get over something like that at a young age," he said. "I don't know when I will get over it, but I'm sure someday I will."

During his sophomore year, Keith had another life–changing experience. His girlfriend, Amy Sida, gave birth to their daughter, Sabrina. Keith and Amy married one year later. Keith was not quite 20 years old.

The two events — his father's death and the birth of his daughter — forced Keith to take stock of his life. He set firm priorities for himself. Most important were his faith and his family. School came next. Keith was majoring in sociology and he was determined to get his degree.

Basketball came last. Still, after a great junior season, Keith considered leaving school early for the NBA. That season, he scored 21.4 points and grabbed 8.8 rebounds per game. Experts predicted he would be chosen among the top 15 players in the NBA draft and could get a multimillion–dollar contract. Keith saw that he would be able to fulfill his dream of playing pro basketball *and* take care of his family.

The opportunity was tempting. But Keith had promised his father that he would earn his college degree. Besides, he thought about the example he would be setting for his own children. "I can't tell my kids to go to college if I haven't completed it myself," he said.

So Keith returned to Utah. He blossomed, averaging 22 points and 9.5 rebounds per game as a senior. He was named the WAC Player of the Year for a record third time. During the WAC tournament, he sank last–second shots twice to carry Utah to the conference title. Keith ended his college career as the top scorer in WAC history (2,542 points). Utah retired his uniform number, 44.

LEARNING THE GAME

That June, the Philadelphia 76ers made Keith the number two pick overall in the 1997 NBA draft, after Tim Duncan. Hours later, the New Jersey Nets acquired

Keith in a trade. The Nets had had 20 losing seasons in the previous 30 years. They hadn't had a superstar player since the legendary Julius "Dr. J" Erving, in the 1970's. The Nets' coach at the time, John Calipari, was convinced that Keith could lead the Nets back to the playoffs. So he landed him as part of a big eight–player trade.

Keith got off to a slow start with the Nets. He sprained his right ankle in the preseason, and missed the team's first 17 games. He could have gotten down about not being able to play. Instead, he turned it into a learning experience. After each game, he sought out Jayson Williams, the Nets' All–Star center. (Jayson is not related to Sacramento's Jason Williams.) Said Jayson, "Keith's always asking me, 'How do you rebound? How do you do this? How do you do that?'"

Watching from the bench, Keith studied each of his teammates. He learned how every one moved without the ball. He learned their favorite shooting spots on the court. As a result, he was able to fit in quickly when he finally started playing.

In Keith's first NBA game, against the Philadelphia 76ers, he scored 11 points. Then he went on a tear. He led the team in scoring in eight of its next 12 games. His biggest moment came in the final game of the 1997–98 regular season, when he led New Jersey past the Detroit Pistons, 114–101. Keith's 25 points helped clinch the Nets' first playoff berth in four years!

New Jersey faced the eventual NBA champions, the Chicago Bulls, in the opening round of the playoffs. The Bulls eliminated them in three hard-fought games. Keith had the flu and couldn't contribute much. Yet the Bulls were impressed. Michael Jordan predicted big things for Keith and the Nets the following season.

THE NETS' NEW LEADER

The 1998–99 season was a disappointment for the Nets. They were hurt badly by injuries. Keith missed eight games with a fractured left thumb. Still, he finished the season as the fifth-leading scorer in the NBA, with 21.8 points per game. But the Nets finished in last place in the Atlantic Division, with a 16–34 record.

It would have been easy for Keith to toss in the towel after that, wait for free agency, and sign with a top team. But that would have been out of character. All his life, both on the court and off, Keith has prided himself on being a leader, on accepting responsibility. He wanted to help make the Nets champions. So he signed a new, long-term contract extension with the team after the season.

"We're a young team with a lot of guys who are going to be here awhile," he said afterward. He mentioned his teammates: Jayson, swingman Kendall Gill, and star guards Kerry Kittles and Stephon Marbury. "Hopefully, we can keep this team together and do

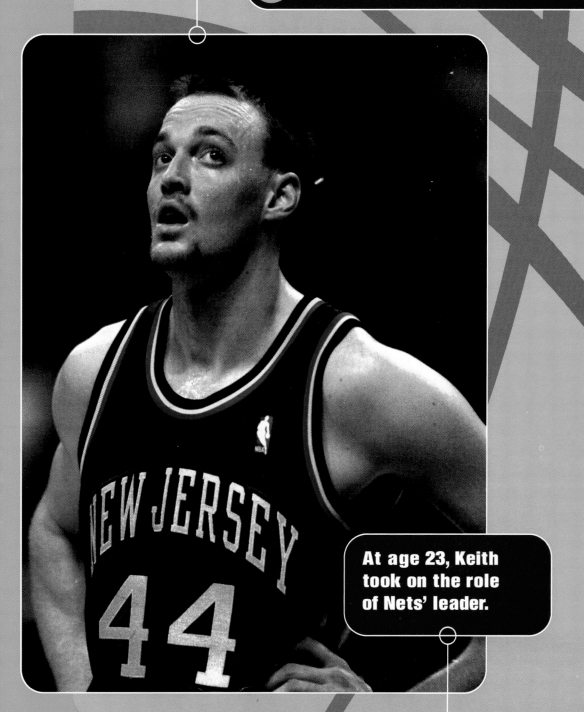

At age 23, Keith took on the role of Nets' leader.

Hall of Fame DOUBLE

There's a lot of Larry Bird's game in Keith Van Horn. Larry was a Hall of Fame forward who led the Boston Celtics to three NBA titles in the 1980's. He became head coach of the Indiana Pacers in 1997. Like Larry, Keith is a clutch shooter who can score from anywhere. Like Larry, too, he has a sweet jump shot and a passion to win. Keith is faster than Larry was, and a better leaper, but Larry was a better passer and had extraordinary court vision.

some great things."

Unfortunately, 1999–2000 was another disastrous season for the team. Once again, injuries and poor play were the reasons for a very slow start. The team never got on track and finished the year at 31–51.

Keith played hard throughout the difficult year. He averaged 19.2 points per game and was the team's lead–

ing rebounder with an 8.5 rebounds–per–game average. He snatched a career–high 18 rebounds against the Washington Wizards in November. Always a good shooter from the free–throw line, Keith also led the Nets in free–throw percentage with an .847 mark. He also set a career–high field goal percentage average by sinking 44.5 percent of his shots.

Keith focused on his personal goals in an effort to help his struggling team. "I really tried to focus on my shot selection, improving my field goal percentage, both from the three–point line and then inside," he said. On his rebounding, Keith noted, "After he [center Jayson Williams] got hurt, the team really depended on me to pick it up and I think I did that. I think I am capable of being more successful in that department."

TAKEN DOWN BY INJURIES

Unfortunately, Keith didn't get the chance to show his stuff early in the 2000–01 season. In an October pre–season game, he broke his left leg, which forced him to miss the first 32 games of the season. Playing in discomfort all year, he averaged a career–low 17 points per game. However, he did show signs of the Van Horn brilliance on occasion, especially in games against the Golden State Warriors and the Toronto Raptors. Against the Warriors on January 6, he scored 19 points in only 24 minutes of playing time. His performance rallied the

Nets to a 97–92 victory. Against the Raptors in February, Keith scored 28 points, pacing the Nets to a dramatic two-point win.

Try as he might, Keith couldn't keep up his playing intensity because his left leg was still weak. "I didn't think the injury was going to be nearly as severe, nor did I think it was going to be as long of a process to get back," Keith said. "I had never gone through anything like that before. My leg was broken in two places and the muscles around it basically deteriorated."

Keith's frustration with the long healing process was recognized by Nets' coach Byron Scott. Coach Scott sympathized with Keith's inability to play up to his usual standards. "I think the first couple of weeks after he came back, it was okay. But I don't think he realized after a month it would be such a big test because of all the pounding," he said.

Even with the hard knocks that his body has taken, the Nets' coaching staff knows that Keith's best is yet to come. Nets' assistant coach Mike O'Koren, who has worked closely with Keith, said, "I've seen him mature physically and mentally. I've seen his range get better. I've seen his defense get better, and I still see signs that he has a lot to grow—which is good. He's not even close to peaking. I think Keith is not far away from being an All-Star."

This may just be the year that he becomes one.

With his leg injury a thing of the past, Keith is looking to reestablish himself as one of the NBA's premier forwards.

JASON KIDD

He's one team leader who would rather pass than score

Jason Kidd of the New Jersey Nets is a giver. Watch him when he is dribbling upcourt. He is happiest when he spots an open teammate. That means he can pass the ball to him and set up a basket. In fact, Jason is so unselfish that, unlike many of today's point guards, he would *rather* pass than shoot.

Consider this play in a May 1999 game against the Houston Rockets: Jason, then with the Phoenix Suns, was driving toward the basket. He faked a shot, forcing Houston center Hakeem Olajuwon to leave the basket to guard him. Instead of shooting, though, Jason flicked a no-look, over-the-shoulder pass to

teammate Clifford Robinson. With Hakeem out of position, Clifford was able to drive to the hoop for a one-handed slam.

"I enjoy when a teammate scores," Jason said afterward. "I always feel part of me scored the basket."

Jason's style of play reminds people of the two best point guards ever: Hall of Famer Bob Cousy of the Boston Celtics and John Stockton of the Utah Jazz. Bob helped the Celtics win six NBA titles from 1957 to 1963 with his ball-handling skills and pinpoint passes. John set NBA records for assists and helped make the Jazz one of the top teams of the 1990's.

But Bob and John were more than unselfish givers. They were team leaders. And that combination is what made them truly great. Jason would be the first to tell you that he is not a born leader. "I had to learn through trial and error," he said. What he might not tell you — but which is also true — is that during the 1998–99 season, Jason became a leader.

SHY — EXCEPT AT SPORTS

Jason was born March 23, 1973, in San Francisco, California. He grew up in nearby Oakland Hills, California, with his two younger sisters and his parents. Jason's father, Steve, was an airline ticket agent. His mother, Anne, worked at a bank. Each worked for the same company for more than 30 years. "That taught me a lot about hard work, commitment, and never quitting or giving up," Jason said. "I also got my unselfish nature from them, which they got from growing up in large families."

Jason was shy, except when it came to sports. He was the only third-grader to volunteer for the fourth-grade basketball team. Basketball soon became his favorite sport. Jason modeled his game after Magic Johnson, the great Los Angeles Laker point guard known for his flashy, between-the-legs and behind-the-head passes. Jason practiced alone for hours at a time, imagining he was defending against Magic.

By age 12, Jason was bugging teenagers at the local playground to let him play in their pickup games. At first they refused. They said he was too young. But Jason promised that he would pass the ball instead of taking shots. The older kids liked that idea because they wanted to score.

Once on the court, Jason unveiled all the slick moves he had been practicing on his own. On offense, his passes were so quick and unexpected, his teammates often weren't ready for them. On defense, Jason hounded the ball handler until he could steal the ball. Soon, Jason was welcome to the older kids' game. "Unselfishness goes a long way," he said.

statcity

JASON FREDERICK KIDD

TEAM	New Jersey Nets
POSITION	Guard
ACQUIRED	Drafted No. 2 overall by Dallas in 1994; traded to Phoenix in 1996; traded to New Jersey by Phoenix, June 28, 2001
BORN	March 23, 1973, in San Francisco, California
HEIGHT	6' 4"
WEIGHT	212 pounds
COLLEGE	University of California at Berkeley
CAREER BESTS	43 points (against Houston, 3-29-01), 25 assists (against Utah, 2-8-96), 6 steals (twelve times)
HONORS	NBA All-Star, 2001, 2000; All-NBA First Team, 2000-01, 1999-2000, 1998-99; NBA All-Defensive First Team, 2000-01, 1998-99; U.S. Olympic Men's Basketball Team, 2000; NBA All-Defensive Second Team, 1999-2000; co-NBA Rookie of the Year, 1994-95

HIGH SCHOOL SUPERSTAR

Jason enrolled at St. Joseph of Notre Dame High School, in nearby Alameda, California, in 1988, he was already 6–foot–2. He dominated his team and the league. Jason averaged 12.1 points, 8.5 assists, and 9 rebounds per game. He was named California's Freshman Player of the Year. Jason's ball–handling skills were so good that

St. Joseph coach Frank played him at point guard, even though he was taller and stronger than many of his teammates.

As a sophomore, Jason did even better. He averaged 19 points, 9.4 assists, and 8.6 rebounds per game and was named California Player of the Year. In his junior year, he led the school to its first state basketball title, and he was named a *Parade* magazine High School All-America.

By Jason's senior year, crowds at St. Joseph's home games were so large, some games had to be moved to the huge Oakland Coliseum. The school sold "Jason Kidd" T-shirts and posters. Jason was mobbed for auto-graphs after every game. He led St. Joseph to its second state title, averaging 25.3 points, 9.6 assists, and 7.4 rebounds per game. Jason was named the Naismith National Prep Player of the Year. His 719 career steals set a national high school record.

Jason could have gone to almost any top college basketball program in the country. But he chose the University of California at Berkeley because it was close to his Oakland home. In 1992–93, his freshman season, Jason led Cal to a 21–9 record — its best mark in 33 years. He led the entire Pacific Athletic Conference in assists (222) and all major colleges in steals (3.8 per game). Then, in the NCAA tournament, he scored the go-ahead basket that gave Cal a stunning 82–77 victory over heavily favored Duke in a second-round game. Cal was then beaten by Kansas in the regional semifinals, ending Jason's season.

Jason improved in his sophomore season. He led all major colleges in assists, with 9.1 per game. He took Cal back to the NCAA tournament where they lost their first-round game against Green-Bay Wisconsin. Jason was named a First Team All-America. After the season, Jason felt he had learned all he could at the college level. He entered the 1994 NBA draft.

THE THREE J'S

The Dallas Mavericks selected Jason number two overall, after forward Glenn Robinson of the Milwaukee Bucks. Dallas was a struggling franchise. Jason hoped to change that. Jason was one of three top young players who were expected to someday lead Dallas to the play-offs. The others were guard Jim Jackson and forward Jamal Mashburn. Jim, Jamal, and Jason were nicknamed the Three J's. Jason's passing helped Jim and Jamal improve their scoring averages. Each of them had a 50-point game during the season. Jason averaged 11.7 points, 7.7 assists, and 5.4 rebounds per game, and shared Rookie of the Year honors with Detroit Piston star Grant Hill. Best of all, the Mavs won 23 more games than they had won the season before. Things were looking up.

Dallas began the 1995–96 season by winning five of its

first six games. Jason began to dream about leading Dallas to its first–ever playoffs. But then the Three J's started bickering. They argued over who should be handling the ball, who should get the most shots, and who should be the team leader. The team started losing.

Jason thinks that if he had known more about being a leader, he might have been able to help the Three J's to work out their problems and focus on winning. As the point guard, he was supposed to be the floor boss. But, said Jason, "I didn't know how to get the team to respond to me."

Dallas managed just 26 wins — 10 fewer than the previous season. Jason finished the season averaging 16.6 points, 9.7 assists, and 6.8 rebounds per game, and was named to the NBA All–Star team. But he wasn't pleased.

Jason realized that his personal stats hadn't helped the Mavericks. Selflessness was fine, but the team needed leadership, and he wasn't giving it. Jason felt frustrated. "It's not my nature to say things or get into people's faces or confront them," he said.

PROFESSOR JOHNSON

Things were no better the following season. The Three J's continued to feud, and Dallas kept losing. Finally, on December 26, 1996, the team lost patience and traded Jason. He went to the Phoenix Suns in exchange for three players.

Jason got off to a bad start with Phoenix. He hurt his collarbone in his very first game and missed the next 21 games. He decided to use that time as a chance to learn.

The Suns were a strong, smart, veteran team. They already had a great point guard in Kevin Johnson. Kevin was in his 10th NBA season, and had played in three All-Star Games. Jason watched Kevin and listened. "Kevin talked about what needed to be done to win and what needed to be said to motivate players," Jason said. "I learned that I needed to be more vocal."

Jason joined Kevin in Phoenix's backcourt after his collarbone healed. Kevin was the point guard and leader, and Rex Chapman and Jason were the shooting guards. Together, they led the Suns to the playoffs. For the season, Kevin ranked third in the NBA in assists, with 9.3 per game, and Jason ranked fourth, with nine per game.

LEARNING TO LEAD

In 1997–98, Jason took control of the Suns' offense. Kevin became *his* backup. Jason tried to put Kevin's lessons into action. He spoke up in the locker room when he felt his teammates were losing focus. It wasn't as hard to do as he had once thought. "It's just a matter of picking your spots about when to say stuff," he said.

Jason finished the 1997–98 season averaging 9.1 assists per game, second-best in the NBA. He helped lead

Jason Kidd

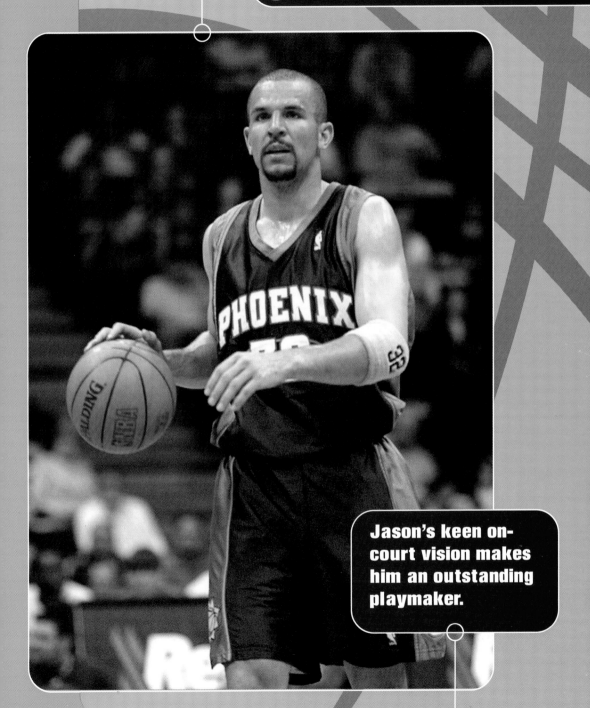

Jason's keen on-court vision makes him an outstanding playmaker.

Hall of Fame DOUBLE

Jason reminds older fans of Hall of Fame point guard Bob Cousy. Bob played with the Boston Celtics from 1950 to 1963. Like Jason, Bob was the flashiest ball handler of his day. Bob was nick-named Houdini of the Hardwood, after the famous magician Harry Houdini, for his behind-the-back passes. Like Jason, Bob led the NBA in assists. But Bob did it for eight straight seasons and helped lead the Celtics to six NBA titles.

Phoenix to a 56–26 record and a playoff spot. In 1998–99, Jason became the first Phoenix player ever to lead the NBA in assists, with 10.8 per game. He also averaged 16.9 points per game. Again, he helped lead the Suns to the playoffs.

Kevin retired after the 1998–99 season, after two

seasons as Jason's on–court teacher. By then, Jason was ready to take charge. Jason's new confidence in being a leader, he said, "has really taken my game to another level."

IN CHARGE

Jason demonstrated his heightened level of play in 1999–2000. Establishing himself as one of the NBA's best players, Jason earned All–NBA First Team honors and led the league again with a 10.1 assists–per–game average.

Jason was selected for the 2000 All–Star team. He was the leading vote–getter among the Western Conference guards. Jason was thrilled that the game was being played in San Francisco, near his hometown of Oakland Hills. In the game, he scored 11 points and had a game-high 14 assists. During the All–Star Weekend, the city of Oakland gave Jason the key to the city.

Jason's regular season came to a sudden halt when he broke a bone in his left ankle on March 22. He returned in time for the playoffs and helped the Phoenix Suns beat the San Antonio Spurs in their first-round series. The Suns then faced the Los Angeles Lakers in the Western Conference semifinals. Jason averaged 10 points, 8.6 assists, and 7.6 rebounds in the series. In Game Four, he had his first playoff triple-double with 22 points, a career playoff-high 16 assists, and 10 rebounds. But the Suns lost to the Lakers four games to one. The Lakers went on to win the 2000 NBA title.

Jason also played in the 2000 Olympics in Sydney, Australia. On a team of superstars, he put up strong numbers, averaging 6 points, 5.3 rebounds, and 4.4 assists during the eight–game event. The United States' team won the gold medal.

IN GOOD COMPANY

Jason enthusiastically jumped into the 2000–01 season, and it was one of the best of his career. He equaled his personal–best 16.9 points and added 6.4 rebounds per game. He led the league in assists with 9.8 per game. This accomplishment put him in some legendary company. He became only the fourth player in NBA history to lead the league in assists for three straight seasons. John Stockton (1988–96), Oscar Robertson (1964–66), and Bob Cousy (1953–60) were the other three players to achieve that feat.

Jason had a very hot stretch where he scored 36, 32, and 31 points in three consecutive games in mid–March. He had never had consecutive 30–point games before. On March 29, he scored a career–high 43 points against the Houston Rockets.

For the seventh time in his career, he was named Player of the Week. Jason also made the All–Star team for the fourth time in his career. He was thrilled. "It's a great honor. This is the second time I've been voted in by the fans, and to be recognized as — I don't want to say top players — but one of the elite players in the league is a great honor," he said. In the game, he had 11 points, 5 steals, 4 rebounds, and 2 assists.

A TIME FOR HEALING

On the court, everything was going well for Jason. But off the court, he ran into personal trouble. In mid-January 2001, he had an argument with his wife, Joumana, and struck her. Jason missed four games as he started to put his life back on track. He and his wife went into therapy to try to work out their problems. "I love my wife. I love my family," Jason said. "This is a situation that is embarrassing to me, to my family, [to] my friends, and also to the Phoenix Suns. I apologize for that...."

Jason also apologized to Suns fans and refocused his attention to basketball. With Jason helping to lead the way, the Suns made it once again to the postseason. In the first round against the Sacramento Kings, he averaged 14.3 points, 6 rebounds, and 13.3 assists. In Game 3, he tied his post-season high with 16 assists. The Suns lost the best-of-five series, 3–1. Though they didn't reach the championship series, Jason was still proud of his team. "This is a gutsy team," he said. "This team plays hard and has never given up."

NEW START ON THE EAST COAST

As one of the NBA's premier guards, Jason has caught the attention of all basketball watchers since he entered the league in 1994. The New Jersey Nets' management were among those most impressed with what they saw. During the off–season, the Nets acquired Jason in a trade for their own star guard, Stephon Marbury. Jason looked at the change positively. "You're never guaranteed to be on that [same] team forever, so you've just got to . . . show your talents every time you have that opportunity to play."

Jason is going to have plenty of opportunity with the Nets, giving them leadership, focus, and — Nets fans hope — victories.

Jason is one of the NBA's top ball handlers.

JASON WILLIAMS

Man of a thousand moves

Jason Williams likes to figure out his jaw-dropping basketball moves in advance. The Memphis Grizzlies' star guard then waits for an opportunity to use them in an NBA game.

Here's one that Jason has practiced for quite a while: He'll race upcourt, the ball seemingly glued to his hand. Teammates will be sprinting down each sideline. In front of him will be a line of defenders. Jason will cup the ball in his left hand and take it behind his back. But instead of passing with his left hand, he will suddenly whip his right *elbow* behind his back and bat the ball to a teammate for an easy layup. In the stands, 15,000 fans will leap to their feet in delight — and disbelief.

Jason, who was traded from the Sacramento Kings to the Memphis Grizzlies in June 2001, has already tried out the move on the Orlando Magic's Nick Anderson in summer pickup games in Orlando, Florida. Former Sacramento teammate Vernon Maxwell has seen the move, too, during Kings practices.

If Jason goes public with it, it's sure to end up an ESPN *SportsCenter* highlight. He makes highlight–worthy plays almost nightly. Perhaps it will be replayed as often as his memorable move against Gary Payton of the Seattle SuperSonics in 1999. Gary is one of the NBA's best defensive guards, and Jason stopped him cold by taking a hesitation step, switching hands, then gliding past him for a layup.

There is only one other player in basketball history who made as many acrobatic plays as Jason does. That was "Pistol Pete" Maravich, the 1970's Hall of Fame guard who was named one of the 50 greatest players in NBA history (*see box, page 118*).

"I'm just astonished at Jason," said Chris Webber, Jason's former teammate.

Even more astonishing than Jason's moves, though, is how close he came to throwing his talent away.

ALONE IN THE GYM

Jason was born November 18, 1975, in Belle, West Virginia. Belle is a depressed factory town of 2,500 people. Jason was a reluctant student who excelled at sports. He was the captain and quarterback of his junior high football team. One of his teammates was his buddy Randy Moss, now a star receiver for the NFL's Minnesota Vikings. Jason was close to his mother, Delana, and his older brother, Shawn. But he was especially devoted to his father, Terry, a West Virginia state trooper.

The Williams family lived in a house smack in the middle of Belle's DuPont High School campus. They lived there because of a security arrangement the school had made with Jason's dad. It came in handy: The gym was 100 yards away from the Williams's house, and Dad had a key. Jason spent as much time there as he could.

After age 15, Jason practically lived at the gym. His parents went through a bitter divorce, and Jason took it hard. Basketball had always been his favorite sport. Now it became his refuge, a safe place away from his troubles. He would spend hour after hour in the gym, practicing alone.

Often, Jason wouldn't even shoot the ball. Instead, he would work on his dribbling technique. To make it harder to handle the ball, he would wear leather gloves and wrap weights around his wrists. Then he would throw behind–the–back passes toward a two–foot square he had drawn on a cinder–block wall.

statcity

JASON CHANDLER WILLIAMS

TEAM	Memphis Grizzlies
POSITION	Guard
ACQUIRED	Drafted no. 7 by Sacramento, in 1998; traded to Memphis from Sacramento, June 27, 2001
BORN	November 18, 1975, in Belle, West Virginia
HEIGHT	6' 1"
WEIGHT	190 pounds
COLLEGE	University of Florida
CAREER BESTS	27 points (against Milwaukee, 12-21-99), 18 assists (against Cleveland, 1-4-00)
HONORS	All-Rookie First Team, 1999

SWITCHING SCHOOLS

Each winter, when hoops season rolled around, Jason was ready to play. During his senior year, in 1993–94, Jason and Randy led DuPont High to the West Virginia state championship game. Though DuPont lost, 79–73, Jason had a tournament–record 13 assists.

Jason seemed headed for a spectacular college career. But his college years were as rocky as his home life. At first, he accepted a scholarship to Providence College, in

Rhode Island. But he backed out when the Providence head coach resigned to take another job. Next, Jason enrolled at Fork Union Military Academy, in Virginia. But he didn't like military-school life, and lasted less than a week.

Then, in spring, 1995, Jason landed at West Virginia's Marshall University. He had to sit out his first season because of NCAA rules about transferring from one college to another. When he finally got to play, in the 1995–96 season, Jason quickly made his mark. The point guard dazzled teammates and opponents alike with his behind-the-back passes, over-the-shoulder passes, and a dozen other hard-to-believe moves. Jason averaged 6.4 assists per game to lead the Southern Conference as a freshman. He also averaged 13.4 points per game.

IN AND OUT OF TROUBLE

After the season, Marshall coach Billy Donovan left to become head coach at the University of Florida. Jason liked the coach and decided to follow him. Transferring meant that Jason had to sit out the 1996–97 season. Midway through it, he grew so frustrated, he called his father to say he was quitting school.

"Jason came home, and he sat here in this house for three weeks," his father said. "He didn't do anything. We have a little 7-Eleven down here on the corner, and that's where a lot of the guys who used to play sports hang around. We call it the All–7–Eleven Team. I said to Jason, 'What are you gonna do, be All–7–Eleven?' "

Jason realized he had made a mistake and returned to school. Coach Donovan was still angry with him for quitting, but he let Jason back on the team.

But Jason's troubles weren't over. He was suspended twice in the 1997–98 season for violating team rules. Once, Jason tested positive for marijuana. A second time, Coach Donovan didn't like the way Jason had sulked on the bench during losses. Each suspension lasted one game.

After the second suspension, Coach Donovan agreed to give Jason one last chance. In a game against the University of Kentucky, Jason showed his thanks. He led Florida to an 86–78 upset win over the Wildcats, who would go on to win the national championship. Jason completely dominated the game. He scored 24 points, including four 3–pointers, grabbed six rebounds, and showed off some amazing moves.

Florida went 12–8 with Jason in the lineup. He was leading the Southeastern Conference in assists (6.7 per game) and steals (2.7 per game) while scoring 17.1 points per game. He was the hottest new college star in the country.

Then, as quickly as Jason had emerged, he was gone. On February 17, 1998, Coach Donovan suspended him for the rest of the season. Jason had tested positive for marijuana a second time.

Jason Williams

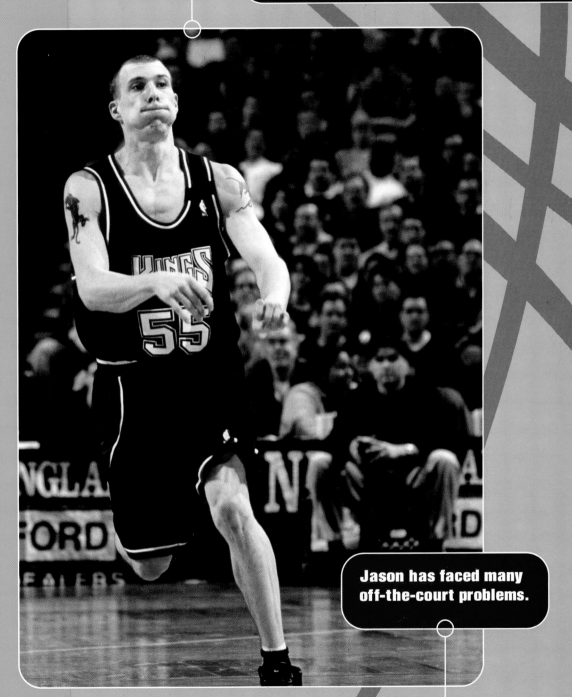

Jason has faced many off-the-court problems.

Hall of Fame DOUBLE

Jason looks and plays like Hall of Fame guard "Pistol Pete" Maravich, who played for three NBA teams from 1970 through 1980. Jason used to wear his hair in a mop top, as Pete did. He has Pete's lean build, and on the court, he has the same swagger and self-confidence. The two are perhaps the greatest ball handlers in NBA history.

"He knew the consequences if he tested positive again," Coach Donovan said. "And that's the thing that was disappointing to me: He knew the consequences and did it anyway." Coach Donovan felt betrayed.

STARTING OVER

Jason's career at Florida was over. His chance to be a top NBA draft pick seemed slim, too. Pro teams shy away from drug users. And since Jason had never taken school seriously, he didn't have much hope of getting a decent job outside of basketball. It looked as if Jason was headed for the All-7-Eleven Team in Belle. Jason's father, the state trooper, said, "I'm embarrassed."

Jason finally realized how dumb he had been. He was close to losing everything he had worked for. And for what? The short-lived high of marijuana? Jason decided to clean up his act.

Jason couldn't return to the University of Florida, so he applied for early entry into the 1998 NBA draft. He might have been a top three pick. But because of his history of drug use, experts predicted that he would slip much lower. Once again, Coach Donovan stepped in to help.

"I could have told all the NBA general managers that this kid was not worth the trouble," Coach Donovan said. "But I told them he was a good kid who made poor choices. A little quiet, tough to get to know, needs to grow up."

On June 24, 1998, the Sacramento Kings made Jason the number seven pick overall. Was he lucky!

In his NBA debut, against the San Antonio Spurs, Jason scored 21 points, had 5 steals, 4 rebounds, and performed a dozen eye-popping moves. Afterward, Spur guard Avery Johnson declared: "That rookie almost put me in retirement."

Later in the season, against the Washington Wizards, he flipped the ball behind his back to his opposite hand, then sank the shot with that hand. In Vancouver, while lying on the floor, he flipped the ball blindly over his shoulder to a teammate under the basket for a score!

Where do those amazing moves come from? "I just play by instinct," Jason said.

COURT MAGICIAN

Thanks to the flashy rookie, the surprising Kings made the playoffs. Jason averaged 12.8 points, 6 assists, and 1.9 steals per game. He also made 100 3-point field goals, the fourth-highest total among all NBA players. He finished second to Vince Carter for the NBA's 1998–99 Rookie of the Year award.

"I think our league needs players like him," Sacramento coach Rick Adelman said afterward. "Our game gets pretty stagnant sometimes. People respond to a little guy out there, showing all those moves. The game is not all dunks. I'm having fun watching him play."

Jason continued to have fun playing. In the 1999–2000 season, he tied for second on the Kings in scoring with 12.3 points per game. His 589 assists ranked him 12th in the NBA. The second-year star had several memorable games. He registered team-highs with 23 points and 10 assists in a 128–110 victory against the Houston Rockets on November 18. On November 21, he brought his

A–game to the Rockets again, scoring 25 points with 12 assists. The Kings won the game 110–105. Against the Milwaukee Bucks in late December, he had a career–high 28 points, 6 assists, and 5 rebounds in a 108–95 victory. A few games later, Jason dished off an amazing 18 assists against the Cleveland Cavaliers.

The Kings made it to the postseason where they faced the Los Angeles Lakers in the first round of the Western Conference playoffs. Jason scored a playoff career–high 20 points against the Lakers in Game 1. However, the Lakers were too much to handle, and they won the hard–fought best–of–five series, 3–2.

IN TROUBLE AGAIN

The 2000–01 season looked bright for Jason and the Kings. With a core team of forwards Chris Webber and Peja Stojakovic, defensive wizard Doug Christie, and Jason, the Kings believed that they had a shot at a championship. Things got off to a bad start for Jason, however. He was suspended for the first five games of the season because he did not comply with the drug treatment requirement of the NBA anti–drug program. It was reported that he tested positive for marijuana. Then, during a game against the San Antonio Spurs, Jason lost his temper with some fans and swore at them. He was fined $10,000.

Jason's game began to suffer. On the year, he averaged only 9.4 points, 2.4 rebounds, and 5.4 assists per game. Jason shot inconsistently and played poor defense.

King coach Rick Adelman knew that Jason's game needed improvement, but he did not hesitate to give praise when Jason played well. After a game against the Minnesota Timberwolves, Coach Adelman commended his player for a strong performance, including the go-ahead basket that gave the Kings a 100–97 win. "Jason made a great move on that second basket; they were expecting him to do a pick–and–roll and he went base-line. That's the type of thing he needs to do. He did a great job in those two possessions and scored," he said.

Under Coach Adelman's direction, the Kings made the playoffs for the third straight year with a 55–27 record. They won the first round playoff series against the Phoenix Suns and then went up against the Lakers in the Western Conference semifinals. The Kings were no match for the Lakers and were swept in four games. Jason's playoff scoring average was less than his regular-season mark — only 8.8 points per game.

A FRESH START

Jason's inconsistent play troubled his team. The Kings expected him to be a more complete player and that wasn't happening. In the off-season, the Kings traded Jason to the Vancouver (now Memphis) Grizzlies, as part of a four-player deal.

Even though they traded him, the Kings recognized Jason's tremendous potential. King assistant coach Pete Carril has complimented Jason by saying that he has the unique ability to see all of the action on the court at once. "This is a skill that simply cannot be taught," he said.

With such positive commendations and a fresh start in Memphis, fans will watch to see if Jason can become the player and the person that they believe he can be.

 Jason's move to the Grizzlies will give him a chance to show off his skills and prove himself to Memphis fans.

SHAREEF ABDUR-RAHIM

The best young star you've never heard of

The quiet man. That's a fitting nickname for Shareef Abdur-Rahim. The 6-foot-9 forward is a low-key player. He has performed out of the spotlight for years, playing for the Vancouver Grizzlies way up in western Canada. Now that he's playing for the Atlanta Hawks, Shareef might finally get the recognition he deserves.

Perhaps playing in Canada is why the quiet man has been overlooked when NBA honors are passed out. Shareef entered the league in 1996, and based on the stats, he deserved to be the 1997 NBA Rookie of the Year. He came in third. The next season, he probably

should have been named an All-Star. It didn't happen. Shareef is the kind of player who All-Star voters gush over after seeing him play. But when it comes time for these voters to actually vote, there's no screaming headline or sneaker ad to remind them of the high-flying star.

The lack of recognition doesn't bother Shareef. "I don't play basketball for that," he said. "I just want to know that I came as close as I could to fulfilling my potential."

How's this for fulfilling potential? During the 2000–01 season, Shareef averaged 20.5 points per game. He also averaged 9.1 rebounds and 3.1 assists per game.

"Everyone talks about Kobe Bryant and Kevin Garnett being so young and talented," said Vin Baker of the Seattle SuperSonics. "Shareef is either better or at least at the same level. He just doesn't get the hype they do."

It's too bad, because in a world in which many athletes are self-centered and filled with arrogance, Shareef is like a breath of fresh air.

LIKE FATHER, LIKE SON

Shareef was born December 11, 1976, in Marietta, Georgia. He is the second-oldest of eight children. Shareef was very mature, even as a toddler. His mother, Aminah, recalls him saying something when he was 2 years old that was so profound, she told her husband, William, "Even grown men don't think that way!"

By age 6, religion had become a major part of Shareef's life. His father is an imam, or Muslim spiritual leader. (Muslims are followers of the religion of Islam.) Shareef became a Muslim, too. He still is. It gives him a sense of purpose. Shareef prays five times a day. When praying, Muslims face Mecca, Saudi Arabia, the holiest of Muslim cities. Shareef travels all over as an NBA player, so he uses a compass to locate the direction of Mecca wherever he is. During Ramadan, a month–long holy celebration that starts in mid–January, he fasts (does not eat) from sunrise to sunset.

Muslim children do not have to fast. "But to give you an idea of the kind of person Shareef is, he asked to join in the fasting when he was six. Now he looks forward to it, like an old friend coming to visit," said his father.

Shareef also began playing basketball at age 6. When Shareef brought home a flyer announcing a recreational basketball league, his father signed him up and then helped him with his game. His father had been an athlete himself. As a young man, he had two NFL tryouts.

William made Shareef practice ball handling with a tennis ball. After that, dribbling a basketball seemed easy! William coached Shareef's fourth–grade team. He remembers the day when, out of nowhere, Shareef did a perfect spin move while driving to the basket.

"At that age, we were just teaching the basics," William said. "Lo and behold, he has the guts to try this in the

statcity

SHAREEF ABDUR-RAHIM

NICKNAME	Reef
TEAM	Atlanta Hawks
POSITION	Forward
ACQUIRED	Drafted No. 3 overall by Vancouver in 1996; traded to Atlanta from Vancouver, June 27, 2001
BORN	December 11, 1976, in Marietta, Georgia
HEIGHT	6' 9"
WEIGHT	230 pounds
COLLEGE	University of California at Berkeley
CAREER BESTS	39 points (against Boston, 2-17-99), 22 rebounds (twice), 13 assists (against Houston, 2-14-97)
HONORS	U.S. Olympic Men's Basketball Team, 2000; NBA All-Rookie First Team, 1996-97; AP Third Team All-America, 1995-96

game!" No one knew that Shareef had been cooking up that move on his own, spending hours in the driveway with a basketball.

MR. GEORGIA BASKETBALL

Shareef wasn't afraid of hard work. He applied his

sense of purpose to all that he did. At 14, Shareef walked two miles for a job interview at a fast-food restaurant. The manager, impressed that he had gone to such lengths, hired him on the spot.

That was a tough year for Shareef. His parents divorced. He moved in with his mother, but stayed close to his dad.

To top it off, Shareef was cut from his high school team as a freshman. But by his junior year, he was good enough to lead unranked Wheeler High to its first-ever Georgia state title. In the championship game, he scored 26 points, 10 of them in the final quarter. He also had nine rebounds and seven blocked shots. Shareef shared Mr. Georgia Basketball honors with Matt Hapring, who later played for the NBA's Orlando Magic.

A busy summer followed. Shareef played for a U.S. national team in a qualifying tournament for the 1995 World Junior Basketball Championship. He averaged 16.8 points and 10.1 rebounds per game.

When Shareef returned to Wheeler High for his senior season, he was almost unstoppable. He led the team to 23 straight victories before Wheeler lost in the state final.

VANCOUVER'S FIRST TRUE STAR

Shareef could have gone to almost any college he chose. He picked the University of California at Berkeley because the school had a solid community of Muslim students. Shareef became an instant star. In his first three college games, he scored 33, 29, and 32 points. Coach Bob Bender of the University of Washington called him "as good a freshman as I've seen — ever." Shareef's quickness and his ability to find cracks in the other team's defense made him extremely tough to defend.

In one game, against the University of Southern California, Shareef scored 28 points and grabbed 13 rebounds to rally Cal to a 63–60 come-from-behind win. "Poor guy probably hurt his back, carrying us all night," said teammate Randy Duck. That season, 1995–96, Shareef became the first freshman in the history of the Pacific-10 Conference to be named conference Player of the Year.

Todd Bozeman was Cal's coach. After Shareef's fresh-man season, Coach Bozeman resigned from Cal. Partly because of that and partly because he felt he was ready for the NBA, Shareef decided to leave college and enter the 1996 draft. Vancouver made him the number three pick overall, behind Allen Iverson and Marcus Camby.

Shareef didn't get off to a fast start in the NBA, but he improved steadily as the season went on. He averaged 11.5 points per game in the month of November, 18.9 points in December, 20 points in January, and 24.5 points in February. For the season, he averaged 18.7 points and 6.9 rebounds a game. He finished third in

Shareef's easygoing disposition and gritty court performance make him an ideal team player.

Hall of Fame DOUBLE

Older fans watch Shareef slicing upcourt to the basket, and they think of James Worthy. James played for the Los Angeles Lakers from 1982 to 1994 and helped them win three NBA titles. He was selected as one of the 50 greatest players in NBA history. Like James, Shareef isn't overpowering under the basket. Instead, he darts and jukes through the lane, opening a hole to the hoop that few players could imagine.

Rookie of the Year voting, behind Allen Iverson and Stephon Marbury.

Shareef was especially effective under the basket, where his athletic ability allowed him to shine. "He can score in traffic, which a lot of players have trouble with," said Vancouver coach Brian Hill. "He can hang in the air and take contact. And because he's a little unorthodox, he's able to score while he's drawing fouls." Coach Hill considered Shareef the most talented rookie he ever worked with — and he coached Shaquille O'Neal and Penny Hardaway when they were rookies with the Orlando Magic.

LEARNING TO BE A LEADER

Shareef didn't rest on his accomplishments. Instead, he worked even harder at his game over the summer. Together with All-Star guard Gary Payton of the Seattle SuperSonics, he worked out every day in an Oakland, California, gym.

In July, Shareef went to Europe with a team of NBA stars. Several older players took him under their wings. "He spent a lot of time with me and Scottie [Pippen], asking what it takes to win and be a leader," said Charles Barkley, who had entered the NBA in 1984. "I told him, 'Number one, you have to go out there and kick butt every night. But you have to accept the fact that it's a big responsibility to be a star. You have to lead by example, to make sure that other players play hard.'"

The experience on tour had a strong effect on Shareef. "I try to draw from all the great players," he said. "I watch teams like the Utah Jazz. They aren't very exciting, but they do all the little things right. That's why they're so good."

Shareef's willingness to study, combined with his off-season workouts, paid off in the 1997–98 season. He averaged 22.3 points per game, sixth-best in the league.

He scored in double figures in 81 of the Grizzlies' 82 games! Despite Shareef's play, though, Vancouver finished with a 19–63 record. Most nights, the young team was overmatched.

THE HARD WORK ISN'T OVER

When his contract came up, Shareef decided to stay with the young Grizzlies' team instead of jumping ship to sign with a contender. He was taught by his parents, and educated through his religion, that good things come from hard work. So, after the 1997–98 season, he signed a six–year contract extension with the Grizzlies. He wanted to lead them to the title, just as Michael Jordan led the Chicago Bulls to the top of the NBA.

Things started to look up. In the 1998 draft, the Grizzlies landed two top prospects: guards Mike Bibby and Felipe Lopez. And Shareef continued to improve. In 1998–99, he finished fourth in the league in scoring. He also had career bests in other key statistics, with averages of 7.5 rebounds, 3.4 assists, and 1.38 steals per game.

Shareef's numbers led the Grizzlies in scoring, rebounding, free throw percentage, blocks, and minutes played. He finished second on the team in assists and steals. His 23 points–per–game scoring average was the highest in Grizzlies' history.

"I want to win. I want to be as good as I can be. I don't want to leave the game and look back, thinking I could have done something more," he said.

A YOUNG TEAM STRUGGLES

Shareef's strong desire to win couldn't help change the Grizzlies' 1999–2000 season performance. The team finished with a 22–60 record despite his outstanding play. He averaged 20.3 points and a career–high 10.1 rebounds per game. Shareef started all 82 games of the regular season and scored in double figures in all but one game.

After the 1999–2000 season ended, Shareef spent the summer playing on the United States Olympic basketball team, in Sydney, Australia. He was picked to replace Grant Hill who had broken his ankle in April. Shareef was delighted to contribute to the Dream Team's Olympic gold medal victory.

But when the 2000–01 season began, the Grizzlies' losing ways continued. Shareef put up great numbers, but the team performed poorly. "I just love the game and I just try to keep that as my mindset. The hard part right now is being on a young team that is not winning. That takes away some of the joy from the game," he said.

During the season, the owners of the Grizzlies were talking about moving the team to a new city. Perhaps the frustration of the Grizzlies' performance and the uncertainty of the team's future began to affect Shareef. In a game against the Los Angeles Lakers, Shareef strongly criticized a call by the referees. It was a surprising outburst from the usually cool Shareef. He was fined $10,000.

Despite the way things were going, Shareef put together another outstanding year. He led the team with 20.5 points, 9.1 rebounds, and 3.1 assists per game as the Grizzlies struggled to a 23–59 record.

The end of the season was very emotional for both the team and its fans. There was still talk about the Grizzlies' move and rumors began to fly about Shareef being traded. Despite the cloudy situation, Shareef played his heart out in the season's last home game. He scored 24 points, had 8 rebounds, and blocked 2 shots. It wasn't enough. The Grizzlies lost to the Houston Rockets 100–95.

After the game, Shareef said, "I've been blessed to play here. I came here as a young man and I think I've grown into a man. This city embraced me and never really had a bad word [to say about me]. I've learned a lot here."

NEW OPPORTUNITY AT HOME

On June 27, 2001, the Grizzlies traded Shareef to the Atlanta Hawks for three players. "We wanted to acquire talent with this draft pick that would make us the best we could be over the next five-plus years. We don't have to wait for Shareef to develop, and he has a big upside because he's only twenty-four [years old]," said Hawks' general manager Pete Babcock.

The bonus is that Shareef will now be playing in front

of fans in his home state of Georgia. "I could not have anticipated a better situation. I'm looking forward to showcasing my talents in Atlanta and getting to know the coaching staff and my new teammates," he said.

The Hawks couldn't have anticipated a better situation, either. They're counting on the hard working, quiet Georgia native to make lots of noise on the court for many years.

 Shareef may not draw a lot of fan attention, but NBA players sure know who he is.

KEVIN GARNETT

He changed how big men play the game

Kevin Garnett is a kind, playful, fun–loving guy who is devoted to his family and to his friends from childhood. He listens to Whitney Houston. His favorite book is F. Scott Fitzgerald's classic novel *The Great Gatsby*. In his spare time, he takes business courses through a University of Minnesota correspondence–school program. In short, Kevin is pretty much a regular guy — until he picks up a basketball.

Then he transforms himself into a basketball revolutionary. He has changed the way his position — forward — is played. Before Kevin joined the Minnesota Timberwolves, in 1995, the classic NBA big

man stayed close to the basket on defense and didn't do much ball handling on offense. But Kevin, who says he is 6-foot-11 (others, including his coach, believe he is taller), does it all.

"Here's a 7-foot-1 small forward who can shoot the ball, handle the ball like a guard, rebound like a center, and play defense like a power forward," said Wolves coach Phil "Flip" Saunders. "Before he's through, he may be the most versatile player ever."

That's a big part of why Kevin was the first player in more than 20 years to successfully jump from high school directly to the NBA. And why, three years later, the Wolves signed him to the richest contract in basketball history. Kevin has come a long way from his poor South Carolina beginnings.

SO TALL SO FAST

Kevin was born May 19, 1976, in Greenville, South Carolina. His mother, Shirley, was a factory worker who earned extra money working as a hairstylist.

Kevin was 12 when he moved with his mother, stepfather, and sisters, Sonya and Ashley, to nearby Mauldin, South Carolina. By then, Kevin was obsessed with basketball. "Every time you saw him, he had a ball," his childhood friend Baron "Bear" Frank, said. "Sun up. Sun down. Up and down the street, all day long."

By age 12, Kevin was already 5-foot-10. But he wasn't

a good player. He was growing so rapidly, his coordination couldn't keep pace. Bear remembers that when Kevin was 6-foot-6 and in high school, he still couldn't dunk. In pickup games, the neighborhood kids beat him easily.

But Kevin kept working at the game. Basketball was his passion. He would watch tapes of his favorite player, Magic Johnson, who starred for the Los Angeles Lakers from 1979 to 1991, and try to copy his moves. People would sometimes spot Kevin alone in a local park, shooting baskets after midnight.

MOVING TO CHICAGO

Kevin's mother disapproved of his spending so much time playing ball. She wanted him to concentrate on his schoolwork. Kevin didn't tell his mother he had made the Mauldin High School team until after the season began. He was afraid she would make him quit. But she let him play.

By Kevin's junior year in high school, he was 6-foot-7 and had at last grown into his lanky body. The change in his ability was amazing. That season, 1993–94, he averaged 27 points, 17 rebounds, and 7 blocked shots per game while leading Mauldin High to a 22–7 record. His basketball future seemed bright.

Then an off-court incident almost ended Kevin's hoop dreams. There was a fight at school. Another student

KEVIN MAURICE GARNETT

NICKNAME	K.G.
TEAM	Minnesota Timberwolves
POSITION	Forward
ACQUIRED	Drafted No. 5 overall by Minnesota, in 1995
BORN	May 19, 1976, in Greenville, South Carolina
HEIGHT	6' 11"
WEIGHT	220 pounds
HIGH SCHOOL	Farragut Academy (Chicago, Illinois)
CAREER BESTS	40 points (twice), 23 rebounds (against Orlando, 12-27-99)
HONORS	NBA All-Star, 2001, 2000, 1998, 1997; NBA All-Defensive First Team, 2000-01, 1999-2000; All-NBA Second Team, 2000-01; U.S. Olympic Men's Basketball Team, 2000; All-NBA First Team, 1999-2000; All-NBA Third team, 1998-99

was badly injured. Though Kevin and others insisted that Kevin wasn't involved, he was among those arrested. The charges were later dropped and Kevin was cleared completely, but his mother decided that it would be best if he went to another school.

By then, Kevin was set on playing pro ball. His mother remembered William Nelson, a coach whom Kevin had met at a summer–league all–star camp. Coach Nelson coached at Farragut Academy, a private high school in Chicago, Illinois. Kevin's mother spoke to Coach Nelson and then moved her family to Chicago so that Kevin could go to Farragut.

For Kevin's family, life in Chicago was difficult. They didn't know anyone, and Kevin's mother had a hard time finding work. Many nights, they ate only rice for dinner. But the family was determined to succeed.

Kevin grew another few inches, to 6–foot–11, in his senior year. He ran the offense like a quick–footed guard, dashing everywhere on the court. But he also scored, rebounded, and had quick hands. No one could stop him! Kevin averaged 26 points, 18 rebounds, 7 assists, and 6 blocked shots per game.

Kevin led Farragut to a 28–2 record and the state tournament quarterfinals. He was named Illinois's Mr. Basketball. "He is absolutely the most complete player I've seen in my whole life," Coach Nelson said. "I've never seen any player who is basically seven feet tall with all those skills."

FROM HIGH SCHOOL TO THE NBA

Kevin wanted to attend college. His first choice was the University of Michigan. But his college–entrance exam score was too low. So he took the test again. He also declared himself eligible for the 1995 NBA draft, in case his exam score was still not high enough.

To most people, jumping straight from high school to the NBA seemed a long shot. Only three players had ever done it successfully, none of them in the last 20 years. Some NBA teams were invited to watch Kevin in a special workout. They were amazed by what they saw.

Kevin McHale, now Minnesota's vice president of basketball operations, and Flip Saunders, who was then a Wolves assistant coach, were two of those who attended. They were struck not only by Kevin's athletic skill, but also by his maturity. "When you talk to him," Coach Saunders said, "Kevin looks you right in the eye. You can see his focus, his concentration. He was going to absorb everything that we taught him."

Hours before the 1995 NBA draft, Kevin learned that he had scored high enough on his last college entrance exam to play at Michigan. By then, though, he had made his mind up to turn pro. Minnesota made him the fifth pick overall.

MAKING THE PLAYOFFS

Bill Blair, who was the Wolves' coach at the time, was instantly impressed by Kevin. But the coach worried about rushing him. So he limited Kevin's court time. Then in mid-December, Coach Blair was replaced by Coach Saunders. Within weeks, Kevin was a starter. For the rest of the season, Kevin averaged 14 points, 8.4

rebounds, and 2 blocks per game. He also earned every-body's notice — even Michael Jordan's.

"If his game continues to grow, he'll be an All-Star in two years," Michael said. Michael was wrong. It took Kevin just *one* year to make the All-Star team.

Kevin could have let his new stardom go to his head. Instead, he remained the same person he had always been. He bought a house in a quiet Minneapolis, Minnesota, suburb. He put a basketball hoop in the driveway and a trampoline in his backyard. He invited his sister, Ashley, and a friend from Mauldin High, Jamie "Bug" Peters, to move in with him. And he kept working hard at his game.

Kevin improved dramatically in 1996–97, his second NBA season. On offense, he averaged 17 points, 8 rebounds, and 3.1 assists per game. But he was named an All-Star because of his defense. "He comes out of nowhere," Tom Gugliotta, a teammate at the time, said of Kevin's defense. "Sometimes, he might be ten feet away from you when you go up to shoot, and then suddenly he's three feet over your head."

Kevin and Tom had taken a last place Wolves team and made it better. When the Wolves added point guard Stephon Marbury in 1996, the team reached the playoffs for the first time in franchise history. Even though the Wolves lost in three games to the Houston Rockets, people began to view them as a team with potential.

A REALLY BIG STAR

That off-season, the Wolves signed Kevin to a six-year, $126 million contract, at that time, the biggest in sports history. Some worried that all that money would change Kevin. But if they had traveled with him back home to Mauldin that summer, they would have seen otherwise. Kevin spent much of his time at the town recreation center, working with boys from his old high school.

When Kevin returned to Minnesota, he picked up where he had left off. In 1997–98, he averaged 18.5 points, 9.6 rebounds, and 4.2 assists per game. Again, he was selected to the All-Star team. And he helped lead the Wolves back to the playoffs.

But changes were around the corner. When the season ended, Tom left the team as a free agent to play for the Phoenix Suns. The Wolves decided to rebuild. Midway through the 1998–99 season, they traded Stephon to the New Jersey Nets. The team, stripped of two of its three stars, seemed doomed. That's when Kevin really showed his skill. He had his best season ever, averaging 20.8 points, 10.4 rebounds, and 4.3 assists per game. Almost singlehandedly, he led the Wolves back to the playoffs.

Kevin McHale, a former NBA All-Star, was amazed. "When the ball is in his hands, he just lights up," he said. "It's playtime. It's like putting crayons in a kid's hands."

The Wolves lost in the first playoff round to the San

Kevin Garnett

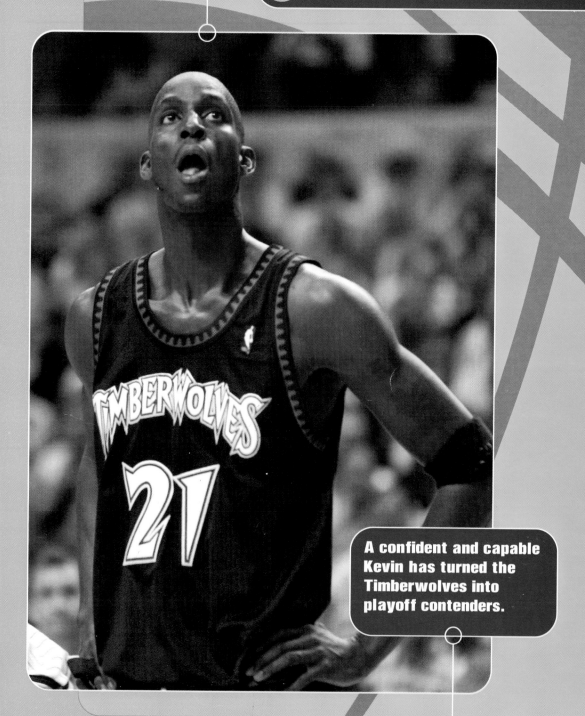

A confident and capable Kevin has turned the Timberwolves into playoff contenders.

Hall of Fame DOUBLE

The only man who came close to Kevin in size and speed was Connie Hawkins. Connie was a star center and forward in the American Basketball Association (ABA) in the 1960's. (The ABA, a rival of the NBA, existed from 1967 to 1976.) Connie joined the NBA in the 1970's and was a four-time All-Star. Like Kevin, Connie ran the court like a guard and was known for his monster dunks. But Kevin is a better ball handler and has a better outside shot.

Antonio Spurs, who would go on to win the NBA title. But Kevin had established himself as a true force in the league.

A CAREER YEAR

The young superstar had an even better season in 1999–2000. Kevin put up career–high numbers in points (22.9), rebounds (11.8), and assists (5) per game. He became only the ninth player in NBA history to average at least 20 points, 10 rebounds, and 5 assists in a season. Kevin even posted personal highs for field goal and free throw percentages. He was recognized for his stellar season by being selected to the All–NBA First Team and the NBA All–Defensive First Team. Kevin was named Player of the Week twice and Player of the Month in January. Selected as a starter in the 2000 All–Star Game, he poured in 24 points to go along with 10 rebounds.

MAGIC 50

The Wolves reaped the benefits of Kevin's remarkable season by setting a team record of 50 wins against only 32 losses. Kevin was overjoyed with his team's accomplishments. "So, fifty [victories] is like icing on the cake with extra sugar, with fifty candles, with all of them lit. And when you blow them, they don't ever blow out. That's how it feels, man. It feels great!" he said. Kevin had help take the Wolves from a 25–25 record (.500 winning percentage) in 1998–1999 to one of the top teams in the NBA with a .610 winning percentage.

The Wolves charged into the first round of the playoffs with high hopes. However, their opponents, the Portland Trail Blazers, were too strong for them, and beat them in the best–of–five series, 3–1. It was a tough loss for the team, but nothing compared to what would hit them next — the death of a beloved teammate.

DEATH OF A FRIEND

On May 20, Malik Sealy, a shooting guard on the team, was killed in a car accident while driving home from Kevin's 24th birthday celebration. Kevin and Malik were close friends and Kevin had admired the older player since he was a teenager.

Kevin took the death hard. "[It's] messed up that my man's gone, but I know he's gone to a better place and that's what's keeping me so strong. I think of the good times both on and off the court. I feel so special because my dream of not only playing in the NBA came true, but to play with a guy I grew up trying to be like," he said.

Many people believed that dealing with Malik's death was stressing out Kevin in the early part of the 2000–01 season. He was called for five technical fouls and had a scuffle with teammate Wally Szezerbiak in the first few weeks after Malik's death. Kevin refocused on his game and earned praise for his efforts. In a game against the rival San Antonio Spurs in November, he scored 32 points, grabbed 12 rebounds, and made two important baskets in a 99–94 overtime win. After the game, Wolves' coach Saunders said, "Kevin played very much in control. He was really at peace and calm out there. He showed a lot of poise." Kevin had come out of his funk.

STILL ON THE RISE

Kevin posted solid numbers for the season, averaging 22 points, 11.4 rebounds, and 5 assists per game. In December, he pulled down a career-high 20 rebounds. In a game against the Sacramento Kings. In February, he scored a career-high of 40 points against the Indiana Pacers. Kevin was named to the All-NBA Second Team and the NBA All-Defensive First Team for the second year in a row.

The Wolves rang up another solid season with a 47–35 record and met the Spurs in the first round of the play-offs. Kevin played well, but the Wolves lost the series, 3–1. During the series, Kevin said, "Hey, winning three games is hard, especially when you're playing one of the best teams in the league. If you have learned anything from me, [you have learned that] I'm not a person who jumps ship when the going gets bad. I was here when we were terrible, and I'll be here when we're great."

With the ball in Kevin's hands, that time may not be far off.

CAREER STATS

 Kobe Bryant

YEAR	TEAM	GAMES PLAYED	FIELD GOAL%	FREE THROW%	REBOUNDS PER GAME	ASSISTS PER GAME	POINTS PER GAME
96-97	Los Angeles	71	41.7	81.9	1.9	1.3	7.6
97-98	Los Angeles	79	42.8	79.4	3.1	2.5	15.4
98-99	Los Angeles	50	46.5	83.9	5.3	3.8	19.9
99-00	Los Angeles	66	46.8	82.1	6.3	4.9	22.5
00-01	Los Angeles	68	46.4	85.3	5.9	5.0	28.5

 Tim Duncan

YEAR	TEAM	GAMES PLAYED	FIELD GOAL%	FREE THROW%	REBOUNDS PER GAME	ASSISTS PER GAME	POINTS PER GAME
97-98	San Antonio	82	54.9	66.2	11.9	2.7	21.1
98-99	San Antonio	50	49.5	69.0	11.4	2.4	21.7
99-00	San Antonio	74	49.0	76.1	12.4	3.2	23.2
00-01	San Antonio	82	49.9	61.8	12.2	3.0	22.2

Stephon Marbury

YEAR	TEAM	GAMES PLAYED	FIELD GOAL%	FREE THROW%	REBOUNDS PER GAME	ASSISTS PER GAME	POINTS PER GAME
96-97	Minnesota	67	40.8	72.7	2.7	7.8	15.8
97-98	Minnesota	82	41.5	73.1	2.8	8.6	17.7
98-99	Minnesota	18	40.8	72.4	3.4	9.3	17.7
	New Jersey	31	43.9	83.2	2.6	8.7	23.4
99-00	New Jersey	74	43.2	81.3	3.2	8.4	22.2
00-01	New Jersey	67	44.1	79.0	3.1	7.6	23.9

 Allen Iverson

YEAR	TEAM	GAMES PLAYED	FIELD GOAL%	FREE THROW%	REBOUNDS PER GAME	ASSISTS PER GAME	POINTS PER GAME
96-97	Philadelphia	76	41.6	70.2	4.1	7.5	23.5
97-98	Philadelphia	80	46.1	72.9	3.7	6.2	22.0
98-99	Philadelphia	48	41.2	75.1	4.9	4.6	26.8
99-00	Philadelphia	70	42.1	71.3	3.8	4.7	28.4
00-01	Philadelphia	71	42.0	81.4	3.8	4.6	31.1

 Vince Carter

YEAR	TEAM	GAMES PLAYED	FIELD GOAL%	FREE THROW%	REBOUNDS PER GAME	ASSISTS PER GAME	POINTS PER GAME
98-99	Toronto	50	45.0	76.1	5.7	3.0	18.3
99-00	Toronto	82	46.5	79.1	5.8	3.9	25.7
00-01	Toronto	75	46.0	76.5	5.5	3.9	27.6

CAREER STATS

 Keith Van Horn

YEAR	TEAM	GAMES PLAYED	FIELD GOAL%	FREE THROW%	REBOUNDS PER GAME	ASSISTS PER GAME	POINTS PER GAME
97-98	New Jersey	62	42.6	84.6	6.6	1.7	19.7
98-99	New Jersey	42	42.8	85.9	8.5	1.5	21.8
99-00	New Jersey	80	44.5	84.7	8.5	2.0	19.2
00-01	New Jersey	49	43.5	80.6	7.1	1.7	17.0

 Jason Kidd

YEAR	TEAM	GAMES PLAYED	FIELD GOAL%	FREE THROW%	REBOUNDS PER GAME	ASSISTS PER GAME	POINTS PER GAME
94-95	Dallas	79	38.5	69.8	5.4	7.7	11.7
95-96	Dallas	81	38.1	69.2	6.8	9.7	16.6
96-97	Dallas	22	36.9	66.7	4.1	9.1	9.9
	Phoenix	33	42.3	68.8	4.8	9.0	11.6
97-98	Phoenix	82	41.6	79.9	6.2	9.1	11.6
98-99	Phoenix	50	44.4	75.7	6.8	10.8	16.9
99-00	Phoenix	67	40.9	82.9	7.2	10.1	14.3
00-01	Phoenix	77	41.1	81.4	6.4	9.8	16.9

Jason Williams

YEAR	TEAM	GAMES PLAYED	FIELD GOAL%	FREE THROW%	REBOUNDS PER GAME	ASSISTS PER GAME	POINTS PER GAME
98-99	Sacramento	50	37.4	75.2	3.1	6.0	12.8
99-00	Sacramento	81	37.3	75.3	2.8	7.3	12.3
00-01	Sacramento	77	40.7	78.9	2.4	5.4	9.4

 ## Shareef Abdur-Rahim

YEAR	TEAM	GAMES PLAYED	FIELD GOAL%	FREE THROW%	REBOUNDS PER GAME	ASSISTS PER GAME	POINTS PER GAME
96-97	Vancouver	80	45.3	74.6	6.9	2.2	18.7
97-98	Vancouver	82	48.5	78.4	7.1	2.6	22.3
98-99	Vancouver	50	43.2	84.1	7.5	3.4	23.0
99-00	Vancouver	82	46.5	80.9	10.1	3.3	20.3
00-01	Vancouver	81	47.2	83.4	9.1	3.1	20.5

 ## Kevin Garnett

YEAR	TEAM	GAMES PLAYED	FIELD GOAL%	FREE THROW%	REBOUNDS PER GAME	ASSISTS PER GAME	POINTS PER GAME
95-96	Minnesota	80	49.1	70.5	6.3	1.8	10.4
96-97	Minnesota	77	49.9	75.4	8.0	3.1	17.0
97-98	Minnesota	82	49.1	73.8	9.6	4.2	18.5
98-99	Minnesota	47	46.0	70.4	10.4	4.3	20.8
99-00	Minnesota	81	49.7	76.5	11.8	5.0	22.9
00-01	Minnesota	81	47.7	76.4	11.4	5.0	22.0

GLOSSARY

berth a job or a place on a team

clutch made or done in a crucial situation

franchise a team in a professional sports league

free agency when a professional athlete can choose his own team

freshman a first-year student; a beginner or newcomer

negotiations when two sides discuss something in order to come to an agreement

therapy the treatment of diseases or disorders

tournament a series of contests or games that test the skills of athletes in the same sport

turnovers when one team loses possession of the ball through an error or violations of game rules

veteran someone who has a lot of experience in an occupation

RESOURCES

Books

Layden, Joe. *NBA Slam Dunk Champions.* New York, NY: Scholastic, 1996.

McKissack, Jr., Fredrick. *Black Hoops: The History of African Americans in Basketball.* New York, NY: Scholastic, 1999.

Sachare, Alex. *The Basketball Hall of Fame's Hoop Facts & Stats.* New York, NY: John Wiley & Sons, 1997.

Sullivan, George A. *All About Basketball.* New York, NY: Putnam Publishing Group, 1991.

Vancil, Mark. *NBA Basketball Basics.* New York, NY: Sterling Publications, 1995.

Magazines

NBA Hoop
Professional Sports Publications
355 Lexington Avenue
New York, NY 10017

NBA Inside Stuff
Professional Sports Publications
355 Lexington Avenue
New York, NY 10017

RESOURCES

Organization
Naismith Memorial Basketball Hall of Fame
1150 West Columbus Avenue
Springfield, MA 01105
(413) 781-6500
www.hoophall.com

Web Sites

The Official NBA Web site
http://www.nba.com
On this site you'll find many features, including: up-to-the-minute news, stats, schedules, interactive games, and links to the official Web sites for each NBA team.

Basketball at Sports Illustrated
http://sportsillustrated.cnn.com/basketball/
This section of the *Sports Illustrated* Web site includes the latest news, stats, scores, schedules, trade information, player pages, team pages, and articles about the NBA. It also has video clips of the players.

InsideHoops
http://www.insidehoops.com/
This site has something for every basketball fan. There are sections for the NBA, WNBA, and the NCAA. The NBA section has features, news, interviews, stats, rumors, and standings.

SPORTS ILLUSTRATED FOR KIDS
http://www.sikids.com
Check out *Sports Illustrated For Kids* magazine articles, try the *Sports Illustrated For Kids Challenge* and send in your art and questions.

INDEX

acrobat, 10
All–NBA First Team, 30–31,
    105, 149
American Basketball
    Association, 56

Barkley, Charles, 54, 133
berth, 74, 87

clutch, 15

Dream Team, 66, 76, 135

franchise, 41, 100, 145
free agency, 88
freshman, 11, 23, 39–40, 69,
    85, 99, 115, 129–130

Hawks, 124, 136–137

Italy, 9

Jackson, Phil, 16, 57
Jordan, Michael, 54, 57, 66–67,
    83, 88, 134, 145

Kings, 19, 31, 107. 112,
    119–120, 123, 151

Lakers, 10, 12, 15–19, 30, 32,
    62, 105, 121–122, 135, 141

Mecca, 127

NBA All–Defensive First Team,
    30, 149, 151
negotiations, 31
Nets, 42, 44, 56, 80, 82, 86–88,
    91–92, 94, 108, 146

O'Neal, Shaquille, 15, 31,
    60, 133

>> INDEX

psychology, 29

Ramadan, 127
Raptors, 70, 72–74, 76–77,
    91–92
Robinson, David, 25, 31
rookie, 16, 23, 26, 66, 74, 82,
    119–120, 132–133

76ers, 9, 19, 51, 53–54,
    57–62, 77, 86–87
sociology, 86
Spurs, 4, 16, 19–20, 25–26,
    28–32, 118, 121, 148,
    150–151
St. Croix, 22–23, 33
Stockton, John, 40, 96, 106

Suns, 31, 34, 42, 46, 75, 94,
    101–102, 104–105, 107,
    122, 146

therapy, 107
Timberwolves, 5, 29, 40, 122,
    138
tournament, 24, 53, 70, 86,
    99–100, 114, 129, 143
turnovers, 57

veteran, 76, 82, 102

Wilkins, Dominique, 10, 36